Bailey and Bishop's
NOTABLE NAMES IN
MEDICINE AND SURGERY

Bailey and Bishop's
NOTABLE NAMES
IN
MEDICINE AND SURGERY

Fourth Edition

revised by

HAROLD ELLIS
D.M.M.CH., F.R.C.S.

Professor of Surgery, Westminster Medical School,
London

With 79 portraits and 179 other illustrations (20 coloured)

LONDON
H. K. LEWIS & Co. Ltd.
1983

First Edition, 1944
Second Edition, 1946
Third Edition, 1959
Reprinted 1964
Reprinted 1972
Fourth Edition, 1983

©
H. K. Lewis & Co. Ltd.
1959/1972/1983

I.S.B.N. 0 7186 0466 0

PRINTED IN GREAT BRITAIN FOR
H. K. LEWIS AND CO. LTD., 136 GOWER STREET, LONDON BY
HAZELL WATSON AND VINEY LTD. AYLESBURY, BUCKS

PREFACE

In the wards and operating theatres, in out-patient departments and in the lecture room, in general practice and among the nursing and allied professions, proper names are in every day use—Bell's palsy, Pott's fracture, Cushing's syndrome, the Thomas splint, Bartholin's glands. Surely every one of us, using these names as part of our vocabulary, must at some time wonder about the person behind the name. In 1944 Hamilton Bailey and Mr. W. J. Bishop produced the first edition of this book in order to answer just these questions. It soon became a firm favourite, passed through three editions and had several reprints. Sadly, both of these distinguished authors have died, and I have had the privilege of taking over the task of preparing this fourth edition.

I have deleted a number of names which have now passed into historical oblivion, but have introduced some new ones—Billroth, Cushing, Kocher, Lane and Lister. The whole text has been thoroughly revised, many old illustrations replaced and many new ones added.

Hamilton Bailey was a great surgical teacher. As a student and a young surgeon, I owed much to his textbooks, which became my surgical bibles. As a mark of respect to his memory I have asked that the Royalties from the sale of this fourth edition should be donated to the Library of the Royal College of Surgeons of England.

Harold Ellis
Westminster Hospital
London 1983

ACKNOWLEDGEMENTS

In the preparation of this new edition, I have received much help from many sources. I would particularly like to thank:

My colleagues at Westminster Hospital, particularly Professor Derrick Brewerton, Dr. Titus Oates and Dr. Tom Rogers.

The medical artist, Miss Anne Jeffries, and the staff of the Medical Photographic Department at Westminster Medical School.

The Librarian of Westminster Medical School Library, Mr. T. Robertson.

Mr. Eustace Cornelius and his staff at the Library of the Royal College of Surgeons of England.

Miss Gill Baker provided invaluable secretarial help.

HENRY HAMILTON BAILEY
(1894–1961)

Hamilton Bailey was undoubtedly one of the greatest surgical teachers that this country has produced. He revolutionised the writing of surgical textbooks and his combination of lucid style and brilliant illustrations has left its imprint on the surgical textbooks of today.

Hamilton was born at Bishopstoke in Hampshire. His father was a general practitioner and his mother a nurse. At the age of 16 he entered The London Hospital as a medical student and at the beginning of World War I, as a fourth year student, he volunteered for the Red Cross. He was dispatched to Brussels and was captured while helping with casualties. He was very nearly shot by the Germans, his life only being saved by the intervention of the American Ambassador in Berlin. On repatriation, he promptly joined the Royal Navy as a surgeon-probationer and saw action at the battle of Jutland. After the war, Bailey returned to The London as a House Surgeon, took his F.R.C.S. in 1920 and became Surgical Registrar. Successively he served as surgeon at the Liverpool Royal Infirmary, Dudley Road Hospital, Birmingham, Bristol and finally at the Royal Northern Hospital in London whose staff he joined in 1930.

Bailey was a tremendous worker. As well as carrying an enormous clinical burden in many hospitals in London and the home counties, often operating seven days a week, he was constantly engaged in his writing. He converted the stables in his home into an office where he employed three secretaries, supplemented by his wife, who acted as literary secretary and helped with the photography. He was an early exponent of the use of the dictaphone.

Physical Signs in Clinical Surgery appeared in 1927, and under the editorship of Allan Clain is now in its 16th edition, 405,000 copies have been printed. With McNeil Love he published *Short Practice of Surgery* in 1932 which is now in its 18th edition. In all he wrote or edited 15 books, alone or jointly.

Notable Names in Medicine and Surgery was first published in 1944, passed through two more editions and was reprinted twice after Bailey's death.

Hamilton Bailey's life was marred with tragedy. His only child, also named Hamilton, was killed in a train accident returning home from school in 1941. Bailey never really recovered and had a complete mental breakdown in 1949. He never returned to active surgery but devoted the rest of his days to his writing.

He spent his winters in his villa in the south of Spain and died following surgery for an obstructing carcinoma of the colon on the 25th March, 1961. He is buried in the English cemetery in Malaga.

WILLIAM JOHN BISHOP, F.L.A.
(1903–1961)

W. J. Bishop was a distinguished Librarian, medical historian and bibliographer. After leaving school, he immediately entered the London Library before becoming Assistant Librarian at the Royal College of Physicians, London in 1924. This was followed by a period at the Royal Society of Medicine until 1946, when he became Librarian of the Wellcome Historical Medical Library shortly before it was opened to the public. In 1953 he retired from librarianship to devote himself to his writing, although he continued to act as consultant Librarian to the Royal College of Obstetricians and Gynaecologists. He edited the journal *Medical History* from its foundation until his death.

His contributions were extensive and included more than 100 papers on medical history and bibliography. He published several books, of which undoubtedly his best known was his collaboration with Hamilton Bailey in the first three editions of this volume.

CONTENTS

CONTENTS

NOTABLE NAMES
IN
Medicine and Surgery

ADDISON'S DISEASE

ADDISON'S ANAEMIA

THOMAS
ADDISON
1795–1860

Thomas Addison holds a unique place in medical history as the discoverer of two diseases, both of which are named after him. These two conditions are Addison's anaemia (pernicious anaemia) and Addison's disease (adrenal insufficiency, usually due to tuberculosis of the adrenal glands).

Addison came of a family of Cumberland yeomen. His father was a grocer at Long Benton, near Newcastle, where Thomas was born. He was intended for the law, but chose medicine as a career. At that time it was usual for medical students to be apprenticed to a surgeon or apothecary, but Addison went straight to Edinburgh University to begin his medical studies. He graduated M.D. in 1815, when 23 years of age, and soon afterwards decided to go to London. Although fully qualified, Addison entered Guy's Hospital as an ordinary student and, climbing the rungs of the professional ladder, eventually succeeded in obtaining a position on the honorary staff. Addison became the first lecturer on cutaneous diseases, thereby establishing the Skin Department at Guy's Hospital.

As a teacher of clinical medicine Addison was very much in his element. His students feared rather than loved him, for he often appeared rude and arrogant, nevertheless they accepted as pure

1

gospel every word he uttered. One of Addison's colleagues at Guy's was the famous Richard Bright.

Together in 1839 they published *The Elements of Practical Medicine* which contained the earliest accurate account of appendicitis—both in its clinical and pathological aspects. They wrote 'From numerous dissections it is proved that the faecal abscess thus formed in the right iliac region arises, in a large majority of cases, from disease set up in the appendix caeci.' Addison also devoted a great deal of attention to diseases of the lungs; his writings on pneumonia were entirely original and of great importance.

It was on 15th March, 1849, that Addison read a paper before the South London Medical Society entitled *A Remarkable Form of Anaemia*. In three cases a necropsy had been performed, and in all three bilateral disease of the adrenal glands was found. There was no mention at this time of pigmentation of the skin, but the paper is of great historical importance, for it provided the first evidence that the adrenals are essential to life. Rightly has it been said the whole of endocrinology dates from 15th March, 1849.

In 1855 Addison published his famous book on *Diseases of the Adrenal Glands* which expanded and clarified his earlier accounts of what is now known as Addison's disease. This included a description of the characteristic pigmentation of the skin and lips. He also announced the discovery of another new disease which is

 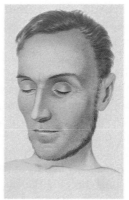 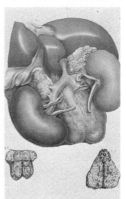

(a)   (b)
Original plates from *Diseases of the Adrenal Glands* showing the characteristic pigmentation in Addison's disease

Addison's illustration of tuberculous destruction of the adrenal glands

Richard Bright (see p. 22).

now known as pernicious anaemia (syn. Addison's anaemia). No cause could be found at autopsy for this condition. As Addison himself states, it was while investigating his 'Anaemia' that he stumbled upon his 'Disease.'

Addison was described as of fine physique, with a good head which he held erect. Within the walls of Guy's Hospital he had a great reputation as a clinical teacher, but, as is so often the case, the medical profession of the day did not perceive the genius in their midst. His discoveries were appreciated abroad many years before they received any recognition in this country.

Addison remained a bachelor until he was 52 years of age, when he married a widow with two children. Always of a very retiring nature, in 1860 he developed melancholia, and retired from the hospital and went to live at Brighton, where he died three months later. The passing of this great man was hardly noticed by the contemporary medical profession and only one paper, *The Medical Times and Gazette*, considered it worth while to publish an obituary notice. Early in his career Addison's private practice was very small, but it advanced slowly, and he died worth £60,000.

Addison was laid to rest in the Priory Churchyard at Lanercost, Cumberland, the home of his forebears. The grave is situated in a quiet sequestered spot under an old yew tree, surrounded by rows of tombstones erected to Addisons and Addysons of bygone times.

BABINSKI'S SIGN

JOSEPH FRANÇOIS FELIX BABINSKI
1857–1932

The life and work of Babinski provide a striking illustration of the fact that research need not be confined to the laboratory. Many of the really great discoveries in medicine have been made by those rare spirits who possess the seeing eye, and having seen, demand of themselves the explanation of a phenomenon that they, in common with their contemporaries and those who have gone before, have witnessed time and again at the bedside or in the consulting room. So it was with Babinski. Extension of the great toe in lesions interfering with the pyramidal system at any point between the motor cortex and the anterior horn cells or the lumbar spinal cord had always existed, but its significance was not understood until Babinski explained how it occurred.

The son of Polish emigrants, Joseph Babinski was born in Paris, and the whole of his life was spent in France. He qualified M.D. Paris in 1885. Babinski commenced publishing valuable papers on a variety of medical subjects when he was a medical student; from 1883 until almost the end of his life he contributed three or four articles to medical journals every year.

Babinski was a disciple of the great Charcot, whose chief of clinic he became. In 1890 Babinski was appointed Médecin des Hôpitaux, and soon after the death of Charcot in 1893, he became head of the neurological clinic at the Pitié, one of the largest of the Paris hospitals. Here he followed in the tradition of his celebrated master by holding clinical lecture-demonstrations that drew a host of undergraduate and postgraduate students.

Jean Martin Charcot (see p. 28).

4

Babinski first described his famous sign in 1896. It was a simple statement that the normal plantar response consists of flexion of the toes, and that in certain cases of organic disease of the central nervous system a similar stimulus evoked, not a flexor, but an extensor response; the toes on the affected side, instead of flexing when the sole is stimulated, execute an extensor movement on the metatarsal. Two years later he gave a full account of this phenomenon in *La Semaine des Hôpitaux*, a weekly journal. With the

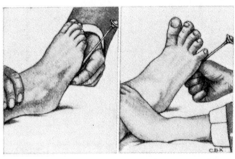

Normal plantar reflex   Babinski's sign positive

passage of time little or nothing has been added to this classical description.

Babinski made many other contributions to clinical neurology. He gave a brilliant analysis of the symptoms of cerebellar disease, and carried out important researches on locomotor ataxia. He paid much attention to the study of hysteria, and was remarkably successful in handling cases of neurosis resulting from the 1914–1918 war. Babinski also contributed to the progress of neurological surgery. In 1911 he localised, and assisted his colleague Lecène to remove, the first spinal cord tumour to be operated on in France. Two of his pupils, de Martel and Clovis Vincent, rank among the founders of modern neurosurgery, and Babinski took great pride in their achievements.

Babinski stood more than 6 ft. in height and had a somewhat formidable presence. He was slow and deliberate in his movements,

Paul Lecène, 1878–1929. Surgeon, Hôpital Saint Louis, Paris.

Clovis Vincent, 1879–1947. Surgeon, La Pitié, Paris. First Professor of Neurosurgery, Paris.

Thierry de Martel, 1876–1940. Surgeon to the Salpêtière, Paris. Son of the Comptesse de Martel ("Gyp") the well-known novelist. He committed suicide on the day the German army entered Paris in World War II.

and was a man of few words. He did not believe in snap diagnoses,
and his examination of patients was extremely thorough.

Babinski died at his home in Paris at the age of 75 years. He

La Pitié, Paris, *circa* 1900

possessed neither the brilliance nor the striking personality, neither
the theatrical flair nor the fluency of his master, Charcot, but he was
more logical and his observations were more detailed and searching.

BARTHOLIN'S GLANDS

CASPAR
BARTHOLIN
THE YOUNGER
1655–1738

The Bartholins are one of the most celebrated medical families of all time. Dr. Jesper Bertelsen, better known by the latinised name of Caspar Bartholinus, and called the Elder, lived from 1585–1629. He married a daughter of Thomas Fincke, who for 53 years was Professor and dean of the Medical Faculty at Copenhagen. Five of the seven sons of Caspar Bartholin the Elder became professors in the university; his daughter also founded a dynasty of doctors. The most eminent of Caspar's sons is Thomas Bartholin the Elder (1616–1680), the discoverer of the human thoracic duct and the lymphatic system. This Thomas was the father of Caspar the Younger.

Caspar Bartholin the Younger was born in Copenhagen in 1655. He gave extraordinary proof of precocity or of inherited talent, for he is said to have edited and published his father's *Dissertation on the Anatomy of Swan* in 1668, when he was only 13 years of age! At the age of 16 years he became a student of medicine, and three years later, while still a medical student, he was appointed Professor of Philosophy. For three years he travelled, visiting the universities of Holland, Germany, France and Italy. In Paris he worked under the famous anatomist, Guichard Duverney, and according to Bartholin's own account, he and Duverney observed in the cow what are now known as the glands of Bartholin. Bartholin records

Joseph Guichard Duverney, 1648–1730. Professor of Anatomy, Jardin du Roi, Paris.

7

this, curiously enough, in his book on the *Anatomy of the Diaphragm* (1676). These glands had been known to exist in the human female for 50 years before Bartholin's description of them. It seems, therefore, that Bartholin's name became attached to these glands because of his clear exposition of them in lectures and in his thesis published in 1677, rather than to any original discovery on his part.

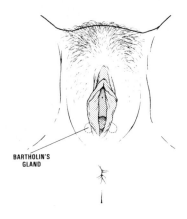

Bartholin's gland

The glands of Bartholin (the greater vestibular glands) are situated one on each side of the vaginal orifice. Each open by a duct about 2 cm long into the introitus. These glands are the homologues of the bulbo-urethral glands in the male (Cowper's glands), and their secretions serve to lubricate the vulva. The importance of these glands is simply the fact that they become infected to give rise to a Bartholin's abscess.

In 1677 Bartholin settled down in his native city, and having shown himself worthy of his name and heritage, he received the Doctor's bonnet at the hands of his father in 1678. He lectured on medicine, continued his anatomical researches, and wrote several books. He devised a new method of preparing anatomical specimens for dissection and preservation. His last, and possibly his greatest, achievement was his discovery of the sublingual salivary gland and its ducts, an account of which he published in 1685. The ducts are still sometimes known as the ducts of Bartholin.

William Cowper, 1666–1709. London surgeon who published his anatomical works in a sumptuous fashion.

After 1701 he become interested in politics and devoted himself more to affairs of state than to his original profession. He became Procurator General in 1719, Deputy for Finances in 1724 and, for his services, was decorated and ennobled in 1731. He died in 1738.

BELL'S PALSY

SIR CHARLES BELL
1774–1842

Bell's palsy, the term given to facial paralysis of uncertain origin, has never been given a satisfactory purely pathological designation, and so today Charles Bell's name is known to members of the medical and allied profession in every country of the world. In addition, until recently the long thoracic nerve (the nerve to serratus anterior), so familiar to surgeons in the operation of radical mastectomy, was always referred to as the nerve of Bell.

Charles Bell was born in Edinburgh. His father, a Minister of the Church of Scotland, died when Charles was five years old. In later life Bell recorded that he 'received no education but from my mother.' From his mother he inherited his outstanding talent as an artist, which was no less remarkable than his proficiency as an investigator. While still a student of medicine at Edinburgh he published a *System of Dissections*, illustrated by his own drawings.

After graduating in medicine, for a number of years Bell helped his elder brother to conduct in Edinburgh a private school of anatomy, which flourished. In 1804, at the age of 30, he decided to try his fortune in London and to embark, if possible, on a surgical career, which seemed barred to him in Edinburgh owing to his brother's unpopularity with the Faculty. Installed in the Metropolis, Charles Bell inaugurated extramural classes for artists, as well as those for medical students, at the Great Windmill Street School of Anatomy (founded by William Hunter). Bell's classes were most successful—so much so that by 1812 he was able to become the sole proprietor of this school. As might be expected, for some time this Scottish intruder's reception by the London profession was

William Hunter, 1718–1783. Surgeon-Accoucheur, The Middlesex Hospital and British Lying-in Hospital, London. Elder brother of the more celebrated John Hunter.

cool, but eventually Bell's unquestionable brilliance impelled his admission to both medical and artistic circles.

In 1811 Bell was the discoverer of the distinct functions of motor and sensory nerves—the greatest discovery in physiology since

The School of Anatomy, Great Windmill Street, in 1783

William Harvey's demonstration of the circulation of the blood in 1628. In 1812, although 38 years of age, Charles Bell achieved his great ambition, and was elected surgeon to the Middlesex Hospital. It is unlikely that any surgeon before or after him has been appointed to a London hospital staff for the first time so late in life. Not only did Charles Bell bring fame and pupils to the Middlesex Hospital, but he founded its Medical School.

After the battle of Waterloo (18th June, 1815) Bell went to Brussels, and was placed in charge of a hospital. For three successive days and nights, with but scant periods of rest, he was engaged in operating upon the wounded. During the lull that followed he depicted numerous examples of the course the missile had taken and the anatomico-pathological illustrations that he drew have never been surpassed.

Bell's palsy was described by Charles Bell in the *Philosophical Transactions* of the Royal Society in 1821. In 1829 Bell published a more detailed description and corrected some mistakes in his previous account.

William Harvey, 1578–1657. Physician, St. Bartholomew's Hospital, London. Physician to James I and Charles I.

This condition of paralysis of the facial (seventh cranial) nerve due to oedema within the bony facial canal is as mysterious in its aetiology today as in the time of Charles Bell. Possibly it is viral in origin. The onset is rapid and is often preceded by an aching pain lasting from a few hours to one or two days. Complete paralysis of

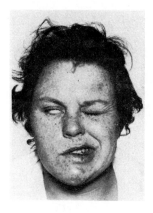

Right-sided facial paralysis. The patient has been asked to close her eyes and show her teeth

the facial nerve rapidly takes place with equally rapid recovery within a week in many cases. Seventy-five per cent recover fully over several weeks but in some patients a permanent defect may result.

Sir Charles Bell's best-known works are his treatises *On the Nerves of Respiration*, *On the Hand*, *The Anatomy of Expression*, and *Diseases of the Urethra*. Bell's versatility and the brilliance of his discoveries in anatomy and physiology were recognised by his contemporaries. He was knighted in 1831, and many other honours were bestowed upon him. After thirty years of work in London, Sir Charles Bell returned to his native city, Edinburgh (the seat of learning which earlier in his life he was compelled to leave because of the lack of surgical opportunity accorded to him), this time to fill in 1835 the Chair of Surgery there. Eight years later, while in his sixty-eighth year, he died in harness.

In spite of exceptional abilities and unceasing application to his profession, Sir Charles Bell never attained affluence. In part, this was due to his devotion to research, but mainly to his lack of business acumen: for example, on being elected to the Middlesex Hospital he disposed of his entire museum to the Royal College of

Surgeons of Edinburgh for £3,000—'surely the greatest bargain ever struck by the College in its long history.' Added to this, he must have lived on a scale higher than his income justified, for when he died his widow was left so impecunious that she was awarded a Civil List pension of £100 per annum.

BIGELOW'S EVACUATOR

BIGELOW'S Y-SHAPED LIGAMENT

HENRY JACOB BIGELOW 1818–1890

Bigelow did not invent the operation of crushing stone in the bladder; neither was he the first to use an evacuator. Jean Civiale had invented a lithotrite in 1824 and had successfully demonstrated that a stone could be broken into fragments by this means. Several modifications were introduced soon after, but all these instruments

Old Boston in Bigelow's day

Jean Civiale, 1792–1867. Created the Urological Service of the Necker Hospital, Paris.

14

had defects. Evacuators were tried, but they were so inefficient that none gained popularity.

Matters stood thus when Bigelow of Boston took up the problem in the seventies of the last century. After several years of patient work he produced a heavy lithotrite, capable of crushing larger and

Bigelow's Evacuator

harder stones than before. To secure removal of the fragments he devised metal catheters of large calibre, to the outer end of which was attached a strong rubber bulb evacuator with a glass container below, into which the fragments were received. He continued to improve his instruments and his final and most successful model was completed in 1883.

Bigelow was born in Boston, the eldest son of Dr. Jacob Bigelow, an eminent physician of that city. He was educated at the Boston Latin School and at Harvard University. Owing to threatened pulmonary tuberculosis he was forced to abandon his medical studies for a time and to spend the winter of 1839–40 in Cuba. In the following spring he went to France, where he remained except for a short visit home in 1841 (when he took his M.D. degree at Harvard) until 1844.

When finally he returned to Boston, he soon acquired a large practice, and to broaden his experience he established a charitable out-patient clinic in the basement of a church. In 1846 he was appointed surgeon to the Massachusetts General Hospital, where he later became Professor of Surgery in the Harvard Medical School.

No doubt through Bigelow's influence, William Morton was permitted to give ether to a patient at the Massachusetts General

Crawford Williamson Long, 1815–1878, a country practitioner of Jefferson, Georgia, U.S.A., was the first to employ ether narcosis. He administered the anaesthetic eight times prior to 1846, but did not publish the fact.

William Thomas Green Morton, 1819–1868, was the first to report the use of sulphuric ether as a general anaesthetic.

The Massachusetts General Hospital, Boston, U.S.A., in 1847

Hospital on 16th October, 1846. The procedure was only the removal of a small lump on the side of the neck of a lad of 17 called Gilbert Abbott, but this first successful use of a general anaesthetic makes that date the most important landmark in the history of anaesthesia. It was Bigelow who prepared the first report on Morton's results.

Bigelow made many important contributions to surgery and anatomy. He was the first in America to excise the hip-joint, and his *Manual of Orthopaedic Surgery* (1844) was the earliest important work on the subject in his country. Bigelow's name is perpetuated not only by his evacuator, but by his Y-shaped ilio-femoral

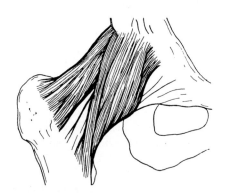

Y-shaped Ligament of Bigelow

ligament of the hip joint which, he emphasised, plays such an important part in reduction of a dislocation of the joint by flexion and rotation.

Bigelow was a terse and epigrammatic lecturer and a clever draughtsman. He was something of a martinet, but was greatly respected by his associates and his students.

BILLROTH
GASTRECTOMY

THEODOR
BILLROTH
1829–1894

Gastric surgery is little more than a century old. It was on January 29th, 1881 that Theodor Billroth performed the first successful partial gastrectomy with gastro-duodenal anastomosis at the Surgical University Clinic of the Allgemeine Krankenhaus in Vienna. Since that time the eponym 'Billroth gastrectomy' has been firmly applied to this operation. However, Billroth was not the first to perform a partial gastrectomy. This honour goes to Jules Pean, of Paris, who performed a resection of a pyloric cancer in Paris in April, 1879. The patient died on the fifth post-operative day, possibly as the result of an early attempt at carrying out a blood transfusion. In November of the following year, Ludwig Rydigier, of Culm in Poland, performed the second gastrectomy but his patient died only 12 hours post-operatively.

The heroine of Billroth's successful gastrectomy was a lady, Frau Therese Heller, age 43 years. Her carcinoma of the pylorus was easily palpable and was producing gross gastric obstruction, so that she was continuously vomiting and extremely wasted. Pre-operative preparations included careful gastric lavage and nutrient enemas. Billroth operated aided by Anton Wolfler, his 30-year-old Czech chief assistant. A transverse upper abdominal incision was performed and an extensive infiltrating carcinoma of the pylorus was delivered into the wound. The adjacent lymph nodes were involved but there were no distant metastases. The duodenum was divided

Jules Pean, 1830–1898. Surgeon, Paris.
Ludwig Rydigier, 1850–1920. Polish surgeon. Performed the first successful gastrectomy for benign gastric ulcer in the same year as Billroth's operation.
Anton Wolfler, 1850–1917. Professor of Surgery, Prague.

18

1·5 cm distal to the tumour, the growth resected, the edges of the lower segment of the divided stump of stomach were approximated and a gastro-duodenal anastomosis performed at the lesser curvature. Billroth used 21 interrupted sutures to close that part of the stomach not employed in the anastomosis and 33 interrupted sutures for the anastomosis itself, silk being employed throughout. The whole area of the operation was mopped out with 2 per cent

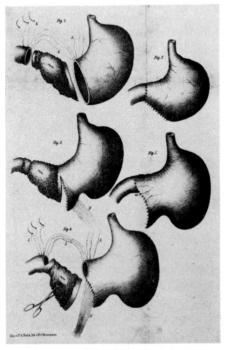

The original diagrams illustrating Wolfler's account of the first Billroth gastrectomies

carbolic solution before closing the abdominal wound. The whole procedure lasted one and a half hours and was performed in complete silence. The post-operative course was smooth. Ice was allowed by mouth in the first 24 hours but the following day teaspoonfuls of sour milk were given. There was little pain and this was readily eased with small injections of morphia. The wound healed well without infection and she left hospital three weeks after the operation.

The excised specimen showed an extensive growth which had so narrowed the pylorus that it could just admit the shaft of a feather. Frau Heller continued to do well for a short time but then developed diffuse metastases in the liver and omentum, dying only four months after her historic operation.

Theodor Billroth was one of the great surgical giants of all time. His contributions went far beyond the first successful gastrectomy. He was born in 1829 of Swedish parents on the island of Rugen in the Baltic Sea, just off the mainland of what is now East Germany. Later he often referred to himself as a 'North German herring'. He was the oldest of five children and his father, a deacon in the Lutheran church, died when Theodor was only five years of age. At first, Theodor's only inclination was to music and he wished to follow a professional career in this field. However, his mother insisted that he entered medical school and he qualified at the age of 23 at the University of Berlin. Here he became assistant to the great Bernhard von Langenbeck, then the leading surgeon in Germany, and proved to be his greatest pupil. In 1860, at the early age of 31, he became Professor of Surgery at Zurich before taking up his appointment as Professor in Vienna seven years later. In Vienna Billroth founded one of the greatest schools of surgery, carrying out pioneering work in experimental surgery, surgical pathology and operative surgery. In 1871 he showed that oesophagectomy was possible in the dog, and his assistant, Czerny, performed the first cervical oesophagectomy in man. In 1872 Billroth performed the first total laryngectomy. He pioneered excision of bladder cancer and tumours of the bowel, performed a hindquarter amputation and, in all, personally performed 34 resections of the stomach for cancer. He founded the modern concept of reporting the total clinical experience of a department including operative mortality, complications and five-year follow up. However, he sounded a warning note: 'Statistics are like women,' he wrote, 'mirrors of purest virtue and truth, or like whores, to use as one pleases.'

His pupils and assistants included Mikulicz, who became Professor of Surgery in Breslau; Gussenbauer, who succeeded him to the

Bernhard von Langenbeck, 1810–1887. Professor of Surgery, Berlin.
Vincenz von Czerny, 1842–1916. Professor of Surgery, Heidelberg.
Johann von Mikulicz-Radecki, 1850–1905. Professor of Surgery, Breslau.
Karl Gussenbauer, 1842–1903. Succeeded Billroth as Professor of Surgery in Vienna in 1894.

Chair of Surgery in Vienna and von Eiselberg, who was Billroth's last pupil and also became a Professor in Vienna; 19 of his own assistants went on to become chiefs of surgical departments. We have already mentioned Czerny and Wolfler, who became Professor of Surgery in Prague and performed the first gastroenterostomy with survival.

In the midst of all this professional activity, Billroth had a happy home and family life, was an accomplished musician (an intimate friend of Brahms) and played a prominent part in Austrian politics as a member of the upper House of Parliament.

Billroth died in Abbazia on the Adriatic coast of heart failure on February 6th, 1894. He was buried in the central cemetery of Vienna, not far from the graves of Schubert and Beethoven and the monument of Mozart.

Anton von Eiselberg, 1860–1939. Professor of Surgery, Vienna.

BRIGHT'S DISEASE

RICHARD BRIGHT
1789–1858

Richard Bright is one of the few doctors whose name is almost as familiar to the lay public as to members of the medical and nursing professions.

This great physician was born at Bristol on 28th September, 1789. He attended private schools at Bristol and at Exeter, and in 1808 entered the University of Edinburgh. In 1810 he went on a visit to Iceland, together with a fellow student, the future Sir Henry Holland. Shortly after his return Bright contributed an account of the botany and natural history of Iceland to the official history of the expedition.

In 1811 he left Edinburgh to continue his medical studies at Guy's Hospital, London, and in 1813, at the age of 24, graduated M.D. Edinburgh. In 1814 he went on another foreign tour, and on his way back in 1815 arrived at Brussels about a fortnight after the battle of Waterloo.

Bright published an account of his travels in 1818 and although the book contains few medical allusions it exemplifies his wonderful powers of observation and description.

In 1820 he was elected assistant physician to Guy's Hopital, becoming full physician four years later. The staff of Guy's at that time represented a veritable galaxy of talent including Addison and Hodgkin, and Bright was justly proud of his position. For many years he spent six hours daily in the wards and post-mortem room of his beloved hospital.

Thomas Addison (see p. 1)
Thomas Hodgkin (see p. 104)
Sir Henry Holland, 1788–1873. First Baronet, F.R.S., M.D.Edin., F.R.C.P. Physician in ordinary
  to Queen Victoria.

In 1827 appeared the first volume of Bright's immortal *Reports of Medical Cases Selected with a View of Illustrating the Symptoms and Cure of Diseases by a Reference to Morbid Anatomy.* The first part of these Reports deals with the most famous of Bright's discoveries, that of the disease which bears his name. The results of further researches on renal disease were described in lectures before the Royal College of Physicians.

In 1826 nothing was known about chronic nephritis. Dropsy was regarded as in itself a primary disease. The connection between dropsy and urine containing albumen was not understood.

Bright's great achievement was to correlate these symptoms with the changes in the kidneys which he found at so many post-mortem

Hard, contracted, granular kidney, which was accompanied
by albumious urine and anasarca (from Richard Bright's
Reports of Medical Cases, published in London, 1827)

examinations. He thus established the existence of a common disease, and showed that it was, in all its varied manifestations, associated with a morbid condition of the kidneys.

In his own words:

'I have often found the dropsy connected with the secretion of albuminous urine, more or less coagulable on heat . . . I have never yet examined the body of a patient dying with dropsy attended with coagulable urine in whom some obvious derangement was not discovered in the kidneys.'

Even had he done no work on renal disease Bright would have been among the really famous physicians because of his other original observations, which ranged over such diverse subjects as the association of diabetes and fatty stools with pancreatic disease, acute yellow atrophy of the liver, unilateral convulsions associated with organic disease of the central nervous system and status lymphaticus.

At Guy's Hospital Bright inspired and directed the research work of younger men, and was always careful to acknowledge the assistance they gave him.

Guy's Hospital in 1875

Unlike many physicians devoted to pathological investigation, he was successful in practice, and was regarded as one of the leading consultants of his day. He was not only an acute observer but possessed the much rarer mental vision and power of synthesis that results in an observer becoming a discoverer.

Dr. Bright was a cheerful, attractive and honourable man, and his greatness was recognised in his lifetime. Today he takes his place among the outstanding names in the history of British medicine.

He died on 16th December, 1858 from heart disease, and was buried at Kensal Green. Up to the time of its destruction in an air-raid the church of St. James's, Piccadilly, contained a mural tablet bearing the following inscription:

He contributed to medical science many discoveries and works of great value and died while in the full practice of his profession, after a life of warm affection, unsullied purity and great usefulness.

BRODIE'S ABSCESS

SERO-CYSTIC DISEASE OF BRODIE

SIR
BENJAMIN
BRODIE
1783–1862

Benjamin Collins Brodie was born at Winterslow, Wiltshire, of which village his father was Rector. In 1801, at the age of 18, he came to London, and joined Abernethy's School of Anatomy. In the following year he transferred to the Great Windmill Street School. Two years later, having passed in these preliminary studies, he entered St. George's Hospital as a pupil of Sir Everard Home. Having been admitted a member of the Royal College of Surgeons in 1805 (at that time this diploma was obtained by passing a single examination of one hour *viva voce* in anatomy and surgery), he held the office of house-surgeon to St. George's Hospital for five months, and then resigned to undertake teaching at the Windmill Street School and to assist Sir Everard Home in his private practice. In 1808 Sir Everard Home applied to the Governors of St. George's Hospital for an assistant, and at the age of 24 Brodie was appointed assistant surgeon: he became full surgeon in 1822. Elected a Fellow of the Royal Society in 1810, he was awarded its Copley Medal in the following year for his physiological researches. In 1818 Benjamin Brodie published his book on *Diseases of Joints*. He was appointed surgeon to King George IV, and afterwards Sergeant Surgeon to King William IV. In 1832 Brodie published an account of chronic abscess of the tibia.

He pointed out that such an abscess can occur in the interior of any bone, but in his experience it did so most frequently in the tibia. When it occurred, such an

John Abernethy, 1764–1831. F.R.S. Surgeon, St. Bartholomew's Hospital, London. His gruff manner was a byword, but he enjoyed an enormous reputation as a teacher.
Sir Everard Home, 1756–1832. First Baronet, F.R.S. Surgeon, St. George's Hospital, London. Pupil and brother-in-law of John Hunter, whose manuscripts he destroyed after publishing the work as his own.

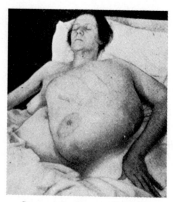

Sero-cystic disease of Brodie

abscess gave rise to 'a deep-seated brawny swelling situated near a joint.' Another condition with which Brodie's name is associated is sero-cystic disease of the breast, because it was he who first described this rare affection in a lecture delivered at St. George's Hospital in 1840. This apparently malignant-looking lesion, which may even ulcerate the overlying skin, is a benign, but giant, fibroadenoma. His name should also be attached to the test for varicose veins attributed to Trendelenburg, for Brodie described this test most lucidly in his lectures published in 1846.

Sir Benjamin Brodie was an astute clinician. His observations are quoted to this day; for instance in extravasation of urine he noted that a black patch on the penis was a harbinger of death. Brodie became the acknowledged leader of the surgical profession in London; few surgeons in any era have enjoyed a higher reputation

St. George's Hospital, Hyde Park Corner, London, circa 1800. The hospital was rebuilt on the same site during Sir Benjamin Brodie's lifetime.

Friedrich Trendelenburg (see p. 224).

and esteem, and his fame was well deserved. A tireless surgeon, research worker, lecturer and writer, he was a man of ideals who raised the practice of surgery to a higher level. In 1843, at the age of 60, he was raised to the rank of Baronet. In the same year he was elected one of the original Fellows of the Royal College of Surgeons. In 1858, at the age of 75, he was elected President of the Royal Society, and in the same year became the first President of the newly created General Medical Council. Full of years and honours, Sir Benjamin Brodie died at his country house, Broome Park, Surrey, on 21st October, 1862.

CHARCOT'S JOINTS

THE INTERMITTENT HEPATIC FEVER OF CHARCOT
(Suppurative Cholangitis)

JEAN
MARTIN
CHARCOT
1825–1893

Jean Martin Charcot was the eldest son of a Paris coachbuilder. He and his three brothers were sent to school for a year on the understanding that the boy who received the best report would be permitted to study for one of the learned professions. Jean Martin was the prize-winter and he selected medicine as his profession. He did not qualify until he was 28 years of age, but soon afterwards by private teaching he was earning enough money to pay his parents for the sacrifices they had made on his behalf.

In 1862 Charcot was elected physician to the Paris hospital of Salpêtrière, and in course of time he created there the greatest neurological clinic of all time.

His demonstrations and lectures drew post-graduate students from all parts of the world. These lectures were prepared with meticulous care and his style of delivering them was most dramatic. Before his immense audiences he stood beside his seated patient on a floodlit theatrical stage. The patient having been demonstrated and led off the stage, Charcot continued to lecture, and from time to time interposed his flow of words by mimicking the various gaits, tics, spasms and typical postures of the neurological diseases he was describing. His learning, quite apart from his mastery of medicine, was immense; he read ancient and modern languages with ease and his lectures were enriched by apt quotations from the classics as well as those of modern writers on a kaleidoscopic variety of subjects.

Among his many lectures and papers can be found first descriptions of intermittent claudication, disseminated sclerosis, amyotrophic lateral sclerosis, the lightning pains of tabes dorsalis and peroneal muscular atrophy. He described the intermittent hepatic fever that bears his name which comprises a triad of fluctuating jaundice, pain and intermittent fever with rigors characteristic of the cholangitis associated with a gall-stone impacted in the common bile duct. He described the peculiar neuropathic joints characterised by gross disorganisation, deformity, swelling, crepitus and hyper-mobility yet with complete absence of pain resulting from sensory loss in the affected limb. In Charcot's day this was usually the result of tabes dorsalis, the syphilitic destruction of the dorsal columns of the spinal cord. As this disease has become increasingly

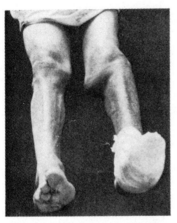

Charcot's osteo-arthrosis of left knee

rare, the majority of cases of Charcot's joints are now due to syringomyelia and peripheral neuropathy, of which diabetes is the commonest cause in this country. Charcot presented some of the earliest specimens of this condition to pathological museums in England and it is interesting that it was the medical profession in this country who first used the term 'Charcot's joints.'

In person Charcot bore a strong resemblance to Napoleon, and there was something Napoleonic about his method of instruction. While he was indulgent to poor patients, his sarcasm was sometimes ferocious and he brooked no contradiction.

He was an indefatigable worker; when he was following up an interesting problem he gave no thought to food or sleep. He was careless of money and often forgot to take his fees, but there was little need for him to worry about money matters, for he had married an heiress and lived in great style. His sumptuous house and garden in the Boulevard Saint-Germain were the scene of lavish entertainments. Charcot loved music and painting, and was himself a talented artist. He was fond of animals and kept two pet monkeys.

Charcot died suddenly from coronary thrombosis when he was in his sixty-ninth year. A statue of his memory stands in front of the Salpêtrière.

CHEYNE-STOKES RESPIRATION

JOHN
CHEYNE
1777–1836

WILLIAM
STOKES
1804–1878

Fifteen years after Cheyne had retired from practice, and twenty-eight years after Cheyne had published his description of this form of respiration in the *Dublin Hospital Reports*, Stokes recorded an account of an example of his own, and quoted Cheyne. Stokes added nothing to his senior fellow-countryman's word picture of the phenomenon. Why, then, should Stokes' name be linked inseparably with that of Cheyne, for so it is, and so it will remain? Having read this short account it is probable that the reader will be able to guess, and the reader's guess will be as good as any medical historian's explanation. Every senior medical student, every physician and every surgeon throughout the world knows of Cheyne-Stokes respiration. It is a sign of such grave omen that much more often than not it proves to be a harbinger of death. Its principal causes are an intra-cranial haemorrhage, both apoplectic and traumatic, advanced renal failure, left ventricular failure, and in narcotic poisoning. By the time the phenomenon appears the patient is in coma. Recorded graphically by a suitable modern instrument the respirations show the following unmistakable picture:

Is not Cheyne's word picture of what he observed equally accurate and convincing?

For several days his breathing was irregular; it would entirely cease for a quarter of a minute, then it would become perceptible, though very slow, then by degrees it became heaving and quick, and then it would gradually cease again: this revolution in the state of his breathing occupied about a minute, during which there were about thirty acts of respiration.

John Cheyne, the son of a general practitioner of Leith, was born at this port of Edinburgh. He attended school near his home, and later one in Edinburgh, but he was a backward boy who took more interest in accompanying his father on his rounds than in being taught at school. At the age of 16 he was apprenticed to his father, and so he remained until 1792 when, at the age of 25, he enrolled as a student at the University of Edinburgh. By dint of much coaching, he succeeded in passing the M.D. examination three years later. Having qualified, he decided to enter the army as a surgeon, and served for four years in various parts of England and Ireland. On leaving the army he was placed in charge of the Ordnance Hospital at Leith Fort, where the duties were so light that he was able to assist in his father's practice. At the same time he attended Charles (later Sir Charles) Bell's classes in Edinburgh, and during the ensuing nine years he made a special study of diseases of children, and published several books on this subject. Suddenly, in 1809, he decided to practise in Dublin, and after two years he was appointed Physician to the Meath Hospital. He was the first Professor of Medicine at the Royal College of Surgeons in

Sir Charles Bell (see p. 10).

Ireland (1813), in which Chair he was succeeded (1828) by Whitley Stokes, father of William Stokes. In 1820 he was made Physician General to the Forces in Ireland. Ill-health caused his retirement in 1831. He went to live at Sherrington, in Buckinghamshire, where he died.

William Stokes was one of the greatest teachers of clinical medicine who has ever lived. He and his colleague, Robert Graves, were among the most famous members of the Dublin School of all time. William Stokes was the son of Whitley Stokes. Young Stokes studied at first under his father, and later at Glasgow and at Edinburgh, and he proved to be exceptionally brilliant. In 1825, while still a medical student, he wrote a classic on the use of the stethoscope. This was the first book on the subject in English since the instrument had been introduced by Laennec in 1819. Stokes graduated M.D. Edinburgh in 1825, and in the following year he was elected Physician to the Meath Hospital in the place of his father, who resigned. He succeeded his father as Regius Professor of Physic in 1840. His particular interests were diseases of the heart and chest, upon which he wrote books that gave him a world-wide reputation. To Stokes was due the institution in Dublin University of a Diploma in Public Health, the first in the British Isles, soon to be followed by one at Oxford and another at Cambridge. William Stokes died in Dublin at the age of 74.

Whitley Stokes, 1763–1845. Regius Professor of Physic in the University of Dublin.
René-Théophile-Hyacinthe Laennec, 1781–1826. M.D. Paris. Physician, Hôpital Necker, Paris.
    Invented the stethoscope in 1819. Died of pulmonary tuberculosis.
Robert Graves (see p. 88).

THE LYMPH-NODE
OF CLOQUET

BARON
JULES
GERMAIN
CLOQUET
1790–1883

Jules Germain Cloquet was born in Paris. His father had occupied the important post of inspector-general of the commercial ports of French Morocco. With the coming of the Revolution he lost this post, but, being a good artist, he was able to earn a moderate income by teaching art. Jules and his elder brother Hippolyte (who was also to become a famous anatomist) were educated at an

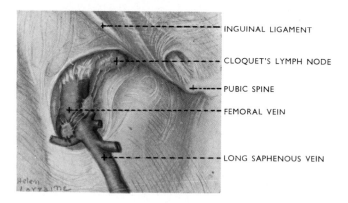

- INGUINAL LIGAMENT
- CLOQUET'S LYMPH NODE
- PUBIC SPINE
- FEMORAL VEIN
- LONG SAPHENOUS VEIN

excellent college in Paris. At the age of 16 Jules entered the school of anatomy at Rouen, and he studied there for about two years. Because his father's straitened circumstances prevented him from taking the full course, Jules decided on an army medical career, for

Hippolyte Cloquet, 1787–1840. Professor of Anatomy, Paris.

34

at that time students at the Val-de-Grace Army Medical School in Paris were educated at the expense of the Republic. As subsequent events proved, perhaps it was fortunate that, owing to a break-down in health, Cloquet had to abandon the idea of pursuing a military career. After some months' convalescence he was able to resume his medical studies at the University of Paris, and his inherited talent for drawing and modelling led to his being appointed, at the age of 22, constructor of anatomical models at the school of anatomy. Three years later he was appointed

The old Hôpital St. Louis, Paris

prosector, and by this time his teaching ability and the readiness with which he was able to illustrate his lectures by blackboard drawings attracted many pupils. As an impecunious student, the Faculty allowed him to take his M.D. examination in 1817 without paying the customary fees. The thesis he submitted was entitled *Recherches Anatomiques sur les Hernies de l'Abdomen*, and was based on dissections of no less than 340 cases of hernia. Two years later he published a book on the causes and the anatomy of herniae, to which authors on this subject referred for generations to come. In this book Cloquet describes the lymph-node that bears his name, enlargement of which simulates the swelling produced by an irreducible femoral hernia. His description of this lymph-node is as follows:

The upper surface of the Septum Crurale is always perforated by small apertures, for the passage of lymphatics, and which are sometimes so numerous, that the superior part of the canal appears to be closed simply by a fibro-cellular net-work. One of these apertures, more considerable than the others, is central, and is sometimes occupied by an elongated absorbent gland; it is sufficiently large to admit the point of the little finger, which, when introduced, will be girt by it as by an elastic fibrous ring.

Between 1821 and 1830 Cloquet's *Anatomie de l'Homme* appeared in five volumes, illustrated by 1,300 figures, more than half of which were drawn by the author.

In 1819 Cloquet was elected surgeon to the Hôpital St. Louis, and soon afterwards he inaugurated an entirely new system whereby the student himself examined the patient and recorded his findings, which followed his notes of the patient's history. Cloquet's classes became thronged with students. In 1831 Cloquet was made Professor of Surgical Pathology in the University of Paris, and he held this Chair for 27 years.

He was an excellent operator, and invented several surgical instruments. In 1829 he carried out successfully amputation of the breast in a patient who had been placed under the influence of hypnosis; this was 17 years before the introduction of inhalation anaesthesia.

In 1840, at the age of 50, his health again gave cause for anxiety, and he toured Southern France and Corsica with his friend Gustave Flaubert, the famous novelist, who was the son of Achille Cleophas Flaubert, his teacher of anatomy at Rouen. After some months Cloquet was able to resume his work. His fame as a surgeon and a teacher spread at home and abroad, and he was appointed surgeon to Napoleon III, and was created a Baron.

With advancing years, Baron Cloquet spent long periods at his farm in Provence, where he occupied himself growing rare plants. Cloquet had always been delicate, and he often said that his life was hanging by a thread. In spite of these gloomy forebodings, he lived to the age of 93, and for his last 20 years, as President of the Academy of Medicine, was acclaimed both at home and abroad as the doyen of the surgeons of France.

Achille Cleophas Flaubert, 1784–1846. Professor of Anatomy, Rouen.
Gustave Flaubert, 1821–1880. Famous novelist. **Madame Bovary** *is among his best-known works.*

COLLES'
FRACTURE
COLLES'
FASCIA

ABRAHAM
COLLES
1773–1843

Abraham Colles was born at Milmount, near Kilkenny, where his father owned a large marble quarry. During his attendance at Kilkenny Grammar School a flood swept away part of the house of a local doctor, and carried a book on anatomy into a field near Colles' home. The boy picked up the book and returned it to Dr. Butler who, noticing the youngster's interest in the book, made him a present of it. It is believed that this incident influenced young Colles in the choice of a profession.

Colles entered Dublin University in 1790 and at the same time became apprenticed to Philip Woodroffe. In 1795 Colles obtained the diploma of Licentiate of the Royal College of Surgeons in Ireland. Soon afterwards he went to Edinburgh for further study. At Edinburgh he worked so hard as to cause his landlady repeatedly to exhort him to take more rest 'lest he should read himself into his coffin.' In 1797 he obtained the degree of M.D. Edinburgh. Soon afterwards he is said to have walked to London—a distance of 400

Colles' Fracture showing the 'dinner fork' deformity
(from a nineteenth-century text-book)

Philip Woodroff, Died 1799, Date of birth unknown. Surgeon, Dr. Steevens' Hospital, Dublin.

37

miles—at the rate of fifty miles a day! He visited the London hospitals and assisted Sir Astley Cooper, then a young man, in making dissections to illustrate the latter's epoch-making book on hernia.

Returning to Dublin in 1797, Colles practised at first as a physician, but soon devoted himself to surgery, and in 1799 he was elected to the staff of Dr. Steevens's Hospital, Dublin. Abraham Colles served this hospital as surgeon for 42 years. Colles early

Dr. Steevens's Hospital, Dublin

became a masterly operator, being cool and dexterous, and singularly resourceful. In 1802 he was elected President of the Royal College of Surgeons in Ireland when he was only 28 years of age. In 1804 he was appointed Professor of Anatomy, Physiology and Surgery at the Royal College of Surgeons in Ireland, and he soon became known as an inspiring teacher. In Colles' day the Royal College of Surgeons in Ireland attracted more students than any medical school in Great Britain; Colles's own audience often numbered more than three hundred.

His name became a household word in surgery following a paper on Fracture of the Lower End of the Radius, which was published in the *Edinburgh Medical and Surgical Journal* in 1814. In three

Sir Astley Cooper, 1768–1841. Surgeon, Guy's Hospital, London.
Richard Steevens, 1654–1710. Regius Professor of Physic, Dublin University (Trinity College). A
    bachelor, he bequeathed his estate to his twin sister for her life-time, after which the money
    was to build a hospital, which, in fact, was opened in 1733.

and a half pages he described that injury which is now known as Colles' fracture. His conclusions, which were based entirely on what could be ascertained by inspection and palpation, remain a monument of accuracy.

The Royal College of Surgeons in Ireland as it was in Colles' time, 1828.

Colles has another claim to a place in posterity. In his *Surgical Anatomy* (1801) he described what was called subsequently *Colles' fascia* which is known to every surgeon as the fascia that determines the path by which urine extravasates in cases of rupture of the

Traumatic rupture of the bulbous urethra with extravasation of urine

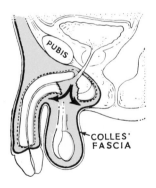

bulbous urethra. Colles was the first surgeon to tie the innominate artery successfully. He ligatured the subclavian artery in its continuity in 1811, when the operation had only twice been attempted in England and never in Ireland.

As a man Colles was generous and modest. He was offered a baronetcy in 1839, but declined it. Colles died on 6th December, 1843. He had a family of six sons and four daughters. His eldest son became a noted surgeon and was President of the Royal College of Surgeons in Ireland in 1863.

CORRIGAN'S PULSE

SIR
DOMINIC
JOHN
CORRIGAN
1802–1880

Dominic John Corrigan was born in Dublin, the son of John Corrigan, a prosperous retailer of agricultural implements. Mrs. Corrigan was a lady of great beauty and talent. Dominic received an excellent general education at St. Patrick's College, Maynooth, a small town situated about 15 miles from Dublin. He was good at languages, and distinguished himself in science. On leaving school he was apprenticed to Dr. O'Kelly of Maynooth, who was also the physician to Dominic's school. The lad showed such promise that Dr. O'Kelly recommended that he should be sent to Edinburgh University. To this his parents agreed, and Corrigan graduated M.D. Edinburgh at the age of 23.

After graduation, being determined to become a physician, he returned to his native city, and started in practice. Patients, however, were few and far between, and to occupy his time Corrigan wrote a small book on the lives of physicians. At length his opportunity came, for a vacancy occurred on the staff of the Jervis Street Hospital, but the successful applicant had to contribute a very large sum to the hospital funds. No doubt helped by his father, the money being forthcoming, Corrigan was ceded six beds. Almost simultaneously appeared Corrigan's famous article in the *Edinburgh Medical and Surgical Journal* (1832) entitled 'On Permanent Patency of the Mouth of the Aorta, or Inadequacy of the Aortic Valves', from which the following is a short extract:

> When a patient affected by the disease is stripped, the arterial trunks of the head, neck, and superior extremities immediately catch the eye by their singular pulsation. At each diastole the subclavian, carotid, temporal, brachial, and in some cases even the palmar arteries, are suddenly thrown from their bed, bounding up under the skin.

41

Never before had this clinical picture been painted, although Thomas Hodgkin had drawn attention to the post-mortem appearances of the condition. This vivid pen picture almost immediately made the Corrigan pulse known in England, France and many other countries.

Corrigan's pulse is often, and aptly, likened to a water-hammer—a now forgotten toy in which water imprisoned in a vacuum falls with a thud at every turn of the tube. This was not Corrigan's

INTRA-ARTERIAL TRACINGS

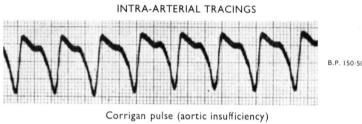

B.P. 150/50

Corrigan pulse (aortic insufficiency)

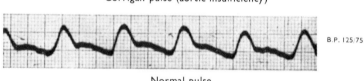

B.P. 125/75

Normal pulse

contribution; Corrigan referred to what can be seen of the pulses of a patient with aortic regurgitation, as opposed to what can be felt.

Corrigan, who was an excellent teacher, lectured on medicine in two of the several private medical schools then existing in Dublin. In course of time he became Dublin's most popular physician; patients thronged his consulting room, and it is alleged that he had a secret door built in his house, in order to escape from the endless stream of those who wished to consult him. Eloquent in the lecture room, he was an astute and practical physician rather than one with profound pathological knowledge. Called to see a nobleman's wife who was dangerously ill, Dr. Corrigan was requested to visit the patient as often as he considered necessary. On the third visit, although there appeared no visible change in the patient's condition, he immediately pronounced that the patient was better. On leaving the house the anxious husband enquired 'How did you know at a glance that my wife was better?' Corrigan replied 'I saw the top of a looking-glass peeping from beneath her pillow.' The patient recovered.

For an unfathomable reason, at the age of 41, Corrigan presented himself as a candidate for the examination for the M.R.C.S. England. At the *viva voce* the examining surgeon asked him 'Are you the author of Corrigan's pulse?' On receiving a reply in the affirmative, Corrigan was shaken by the hand and was awarded the diploma without further interrogation. On another occasion Corrigan, who was very fond of foreign travel, attended a ward round at the Hôtel Dieu in Paris. In the allotted space upon the bed-board of one of the patients that the class visited was inscribed 'Maladie de Corrigan.' 'Do you know Corrigan of Dublin?' asked the physician in charge. 'C'est moi, Monsieur,' was the prompt reply. After demonstrating this patient, the physician in charge requested the class to follow him into the lecture theatre, where he introduced his distinguished guest to the students amid loud acclamation. Corrigan was not elected an Honorary Fellow of the Irish College of Physicians until he was 52 years of age (1854).

Corrigan's unmitigated success in every project he undertook was not upheld when he was returned Member of Parliament for Dublin; indeed, he was described as a failure at Westminster. Apart from his first paper, he has left no other work of note, but his eloquence is remembered to this day by one passage of his Presidential Address to the British Medical Association meeting in Dublin in 1867. 'Among the bonds that unite members of our profession none are stronger than those that cause us to soar above all sectarian discord: we know no differences of race, creed or colour. Every man is our neighbour.'

In the year previous to this oration he had been created a Baronet, and in 1870 he was appointed Physician-in-ordinary to Queen Victoria in Ireland. In his later years Sir Dominic suffered from gout and a high blood-pressure, and he died suddenly following a massive cerebral haemorrhage.

COURVOISIER'S LAW

LUDWIG
COURVOISIER
1843–1918

Courvoisier's law states 'If in the presence of jaundice the gall-bladder is palpable, then the jaundice is unlikely to be due to stone'. This is an extremely useful rule providing it is enunciated correctly. The principle on which it is based is that, if the obstruction is due to stone, the gall-bladder is usually thickened

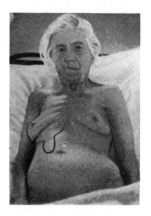

Patient with advanced obstructive jaundice due to carcinoma of the head of the pancreas. The gall-bladder is enlarged

and fibrotic and therefore does not distend. Moreover, the obstruction is usually incomplete and so some bile is able to escape from the biliary system. Obstruction of the common bile duct due to other causes, of which the commonest is carcinoma of the head of the pancreas, is usually associated with a normal gall-bladder which

44

can dilate. Note that the law is not phrased the other way round—
'if the gall-bladder is *not* palpable the jaundice is due to stone'—
since 50 per cent of dilated gall-bladders cannot be palpated on
clinical examination, due either to the patient's obesity or because
of overlap by the liver, which itself is usually enlarged as a result of
bile engorgement.

This 'law' was first put forward by Courvoisier in his book on
The Pathology and Surgery of the Gall-Bladder, published at
Leipzig in 1890; it was a work based on over 450 personal operations
on the gall-bladder and bile-passages.

The Old Bürgerspital, Basle

Ludwig Courvoisier was born at Basle, Switzerland. His father
was a merchant and his mother was the daughter of an English
clergyman. At the age of seven he went with his parents to Malta,
the reasons being that his father developed pulmonary tuberculosis
and his maternal grandparents lived there. Thus he acquired an
excellent knowledge of English. As a boy he was extremely fond of
natural history, and spent much of his spare time in botanising and
hunting butterlies. As he was about to enter the university as a
medical student, Courvoisier was stricken with typhus, and was so
ill that he could not commence his studies for over a year. When he
did enrol, he soon overtook his contemporaries, and won many
prizes. His final undergraduate years were spent at the University

of Göttingen, and he returned to his native city to graduate M.D. Basle in 1868. Soon afterwards, at the age of 25, he was chosen by Professor Socin to act as his assistant. Socin was one of the first Continental surgeons to adopt the antiseptic method. At the end of his assistantship Courvoisier visited London, and studied under Sir William Fergusson and Sir Spencer Wells. He then spent a year in Vienna, where he followed the work of Billroth and Czerny. To the end of his long life he spoke with affection and gratitude of these great men, and especially of his teacher Socin.

During the Franco-Prussian war Courvoisier served in a military hospital at Karlsruhe. After the war he returned to Basle, and soon afterwards he was elected surgeon to a hospital in Riehen, a small town about five miles north-east of Basle on the German-Swiss border. For 30 years this was the scene of his labours. His reputation as a surgeon spread far and wide, and within 10 years of his commencing practice in Riehen he was admitted as a recognised teacher of surgery in the University of Basle. While still only on the staff of the small hospital at Riehen, he went to reside in Basle in 1883, and started a private clinic there, which was most successful. In 1888 the university recognised his work, and accorded him the title of Professor of Surgery Extraordinary. It was not until the death of Socin in 1899, when Courvoisier was 57 years of age, that he was allotted any hospital beds in Basle, and shortly afterwards he was elected Professor of Surgery in the University.

Courvoisier's most important work was concerned with the biliary tract, and he was the virtual founder of this branch of surgery. It was he who popularised the operation of cholecystectomy, and he was one of the first to remove a stone from the common bile-duct. These accomplishments gave him an international reputation.

A safe, rather than a brilliant, operator, he gladly handed over the case to others when confronted with conditions lying outside his experience. Courvoisier never abandoned his boyhood's love of flowers and butterflies, and in addition to his surgical writings he published 21 papers on entomology. He bequeathed his great

August Socin, 1839–1899. Professor of Surgery, Basle.
Sir William Fergusson (see p. 71).
Sir Thomas Spencer Wells (see p. 237).
Theodor Billroth (see p. 18).
Vincenz Czerny, 1842–1916. Sometime first assistant to Professor Billroth, and later Professor of Surgery at Heidelberg.

herbarium to the Botanical Institute, and his collection of butterflies to the Natural History Museum of Basle.

Courvoisier died at the age of 75, and is rightly regarded as the
first of a line of famous abdominal surgeons of Basle.

MILLICURIE (mC.)
MICROCURIE (μC)

MARIE
CURIE
1867–1934

The unit of radio-activity is the curie. A curie is too large a unit for purposes of treatment by an isotope, consequently such doses are expressed in millicuries (mCi) or microcuries (μCi), these being a thousandth and a millionth part of a curie respectively.

The curie is so-named in honour of Pierre and Marie Curie.

Marie Sklodowska was a Pole. She was born in Warsaw, the youngest child of a family of five. Her father was a teacher of mathematics and physics, and had a hard struggle to keep together a home on his slender stipend. When Marie was nine her mother died, and this tragedy no doubt helped to develop that wonderful power of overcoming difficulties that characterised Marie Sklodowska's whole life.

At the age of 17, Marie became governess to a landed gentleman's children. She held this post for five years, but all the time she longed to study science, a bent which she must have inherited from her father.

Out of her salary she saved enough to take her to Paris, where she enrolled as a student. Her funds were so inadequate that she suffered great hardships, living in an attic without proper food or fuel. She worked at the university during the day and studied in her attic far into the night, preparing for examinations at which she was brilliantly successful.

Then she met Pierre Curie.* A year later (1895) they married, and Marie worked in her husband's laboratory. Thus began the partnership which has so enriched the world.

About this time Becquerel noted that the salts of the metal uranium emitted rays. The Curies became interested in this subject. They procured some uranium and began experimenting in an old shed, which they had converted into a primitive laboratory. Two years later they announced the discovery of two new elements— radium and polonium—which they had isolated from mineral pitchblendes. Polonium was so named by Madame Curie in commemoration of her native Poland.

Stamp commemorating the 40th anniversary of the discovery of radium

Recognition and honours now came to the Curies. In 1903 the Nobel Prize in physics was awarded to them jointly with Becquerel (in 1911 she was to receive the Nobel Prize for a second time, on this occasion alone). At the very moment when the fame of the two scientists and benefactors was spreading throughout the world, a tragic accident robbed Madame Curie of her wonderful companion. Pierre Curie was run over in a Paris street and killed. Madame Curie never completely recovered from this blow, though she continued to develop the science they had created together with unprecedented brilliance.

She succeeded her husband as Professor of Physics at the university, and was the first woman to hold such a position there. At her inaugural lecture she resumed the course at the precise sentence where Pierre Curie had left it. The University of Paris created a Radium Institute and placed Madame Curie at the head of the research department. This she directed until a few weeks before her death.

* Pierre Curie (1859–1906) was at this time 35 years of age and was Chief of the Laboratory at the School of Physics and Chemistry of the City of Paris.

Antoine Henri Becquerel, 1852–1908. Professor of Physics at the École Polytechnique, Paris.

In 1921 she visited the United States to receive a gramme of radium presented to her by the President. In 1929 she paid a second visit to the New World, this time to accept a cheque for 50,000 dollars subscribed by American funds. This sum of money she gave to her native city of Warsaw for the promotion of research in radium.

Madame Curie in her laboratory

Madame Curie died of aplastic anaemia at the age of 66 years. There is little doubt that the long exposure to radiation caused this fell disease that hastened her end. The Curies had two daughters, Irène and Eve. Before she died Madame Curie had the happiness of seeing her work continued by Irène and her husband, M. Joliot.

Jean Frédéric Joliot-Curie, 1900–1958. Physicist. Professor at the Collège de France. High Commissioner for Atomic Energy in France, 1945–1950.

CUSHING'S SYNDROME

HARVEY WILLIAMS CUSHING 1869–1939

Those who believe that surgeons should be painlessly put down at the age of 60 might reflect that Harvey Cushing's important contribution was made when he was in his 63rd year!

We now know that the clinical manifestations of the syndrome result from excessive production of cortisol by the adrenal cortex. The majority of cases result from hyperplasia of the adrenal cortex but about 10 per cent are due to benign or malignant cortical tumours or rarely a basophil adenoma of the pituitary. Many examples of the syndrome nowadays are iatrogenic, resulting from the therapeutic administration of steroids.

Cushing had been interested in diseases of the pituitary for most of his professional life and in 1912 published a monograph, *The Pituitary Body and its Disorders*, with 47 carefully documented cases. One at least of these was a typical example of this syndrome. Over the years he observed a number of such cases, which he vaguely labelled 'polyglandular syndrome'. Since they did not develop visual difficulty or signs of increased intra-cranial pressure they were seldom subjected to operation and none had come to post mortem examination, so it was not until 1932 that he was able to describe the association of a basophilic tumour of the pituitary with this clinical syndrome.

The clinical features are most striking. The syndrome usually affects young adults, females more than males. There is adiposity with central distribution, abdominal striae, a red moon-face and diabetes. There may be osteoporosis, leading to vertebral collapse.

51

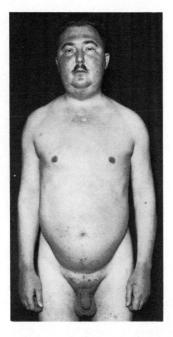

Cushing's syndrome. Note the typical 'moon-face'

Other features are hypertension, hirsutism and acne, with amenor-
rhoea in the female or impotence in the male.

Harvey Cushing, one of the founders of modern neurosurgery,
was born in Cleveland, Ohio. His father was Professor of Obstetrics
and his grandfather and great-grandfather had also been doctors.
He graduated in medicine at Harvard University in 1895 and after
internship in Boston went to the John Hopkins Hospital in
Baltimore as assistant to William Halsted. It was at this time that
he came under the influence of William Osler, whose biography he
was eventually to write in 1925 and for which he was awarded the
Pulitzer Prize.

In Baltimore, Cushing gradually concentrated his interests on
the surgery of the brain and specialised entirely in this from 1902
onwards. In 1912 he became Professor of Surgery in the Harvard
Medical School in Boston and over the next 20 years at the Peter

William S. Halsted, 1852–1922. Surgeon at the Johns Hopkins Hospital, Baltimore. Carried out
    pioneer work on the use of cocaine in local anaesthesia and popularised radical mastectomy.
    In the USA this is referred to as the Halsted operation.
William Osler, 1849–1919. Canadian by birth. Successively Professor of Medicine in Philadelphia,
    Baltimore and Oxford.

Cushing's clips

Bent Brigham Hospital he established a school of neurosurgery whose disciples spread throughout the world. At the end of his career, he was operating on some 200 brain tumours annually.

As a surgeon, he was a perfectionist. He worked slowly and in complete silence; a craniotomy might take up to six hours. He devised many of the techniques still in standard neurosurgical use today. These included the use of suction to maintain a clear field, the application of the electro-cautery devised by Bovie, and the use of silver clips, which now bear his name, to clip cerebral vessels.

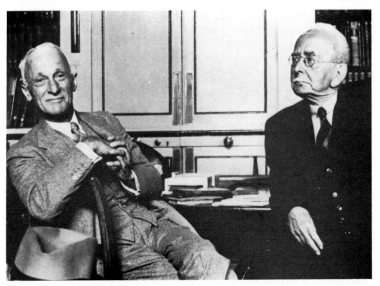

Cushing with Sir Charles Sherrington, the distinguished neuro-physiologist, at the Royal College of Surgeons

William T. Bovie, 1882–1958. Devised the electro-cautery unit used by Cushing for the first time On October 1st 1926. In the USA the diathermy apparatus is often still termed the Bovie unit. He later became Professor of Biophysics at the North Western University, Chicago.

During World War I, he served in an American unit as a neurosurgeon before his country entered the War. He then returned to France in 1917 as an army neurosurgeon, becoming senior consultant in neurosurgery to the American Expeditionary Force. For his services to the British army he was made a military Companion of the Bath in 1919.

He was a prolific writer. In addition to the books already mentioned he wrote monographs on acoustic tumours, on meningiomas, and on classification of gliomas. In 1932 he published a report on 2000 consecutive intra-cranial tumours. He was also a medical historian and published a biobibliography of Vesalius. In all he wrote 13 books and over 300 articles. He was a skilled draftsman and many of his contributions were illustrated with his own magnificent drawings.

Cushing retired from active neurosurgical practice in 1932, the year that he documented his syndrome, and returned to Yale as Professor of Neurology. In the last two years of his life, failing health made him resign from this appointment and he died of a coronary thrombosis on the 7th October 1939.

DOVER'S POWDER

THOMAS DOVER
1660–1742

Thomas Dover rescues Alexander
Selkirk from the island of Juan
Fernandez. This was during Dover's
career as a pirate

Dover's Powder is a diaphoretic and sedative, containing 10 per
cent each of opium and ipecacuanha, the bulk of the powder being
made up by lactose. There is nothing in this official text-book
definition to suggest the romantic story attached to this famous
remedy, which has been prescribed in feverish conditions for over
two hundred years.

Dover's Powder was the invention of Captain Thomas Dover,
bachelor of medicine, sometime pirate on the Spanish Main, and
one of the most amazing figures in medical history. Dover was born
in Warwickshire about 1660. He took his M.B. degree at Cambridge
and shortly afterwards became a resident pupil of the famous Dr.
Thomas Sydenham in London. Soon after moving to London, the
newly qualified Dr. Dover contracted smallpox, and he has left an
interesting description of the treatment he received at the hands of
Dr. Sydenham:

'In the beginning I lost twenty-two ounces of blood. He gave me
a vomit; but I find by experience purging much better. I went
abroad, by his direction, till I was blind, and then took to my bed.
I had no fire allowed in my room: my windows were constantly

*Thomas Sydenham, 1624–1689. His fame rests on his accounts of gout, scarlet fever, measles, and
the malarial fevers of his time. He had no hospital appointment.*

open, my bed clothes were order'd to be laid no higher than my waist. He made me take twelve bottles of small beer, acidulated with spirit of vitriol, every twenty-four hours.'

In later life Dover was very proud of his association with Sydenham, and he makes frequent reference to his old master in his writings.

Presently Dover started practice in Bristol and achieved distinction as the first medical man to give free attendance on the sick poor of the city. In 1696 he showed great zeal and courage during an epidemic of spotted fever. In 1708, having amassed sufficient capital, he became a partner in a pirateering expedition to the South Seas at a time when the plundering of Spanish ships and colonies was regarded as the rightful prerogative of Englishmen.

In addition to acting as the ship's doctor, Dover took his full share in the fighting, and led a successful attack on the city of Guayaquil in Ecuador. The most noted event of the expedition took place on 2nd February, 1709, when Dover rescued from the island of Juan Fernandez, off the coast of Chile, a ship-wrecked Scottish sailor named Alexander Selkirk, who had lived there alone for over four years. The adventurers returned to England in 1711 with booty to the value of £170,000, and, what is more important

Statue of Alexander Selkirk at Lower Largo, Fifeshire

Stanway House, Gloucestershire. Thomas
Dover's last residence. (*Bodleian Library,
Oxford*)

to us, brought back Alexander Selkirk. Captain Woodes Rogers,
the commander of the ship in which Dover sailed, published a full
account of the expedition in a book entitled *A Cruising Voyage
Round the World*, and it was upon the story of Alexander Selkirk
as related therein that Daniel Defoe based the immortal story of
Robinson Crusoe.

Resuming medical practice, Dover was admitted a Licentiate of
the College of Physicians in 1721 and settled in London, still
retaining however many of his piratical ways. In 1732 he published
a book, *The Ancient Physician's Legacy to his Country*, in which he
gave a long recital of marvellous cures, all attesting his superlative
skill in physic, and made a violent attack on the apothecaries, the
general practitioners of that day.

It was in this book that Dover gave the formula of his famous
powder:

Take Opium one ounce, Salt-Petre and Tartar vitriolated each four ounces,
Ipecacuanha one ounce. Put the Salt-Petre and Tartar into a red hot mortar, stirring
them with a spoon until they have done flaming. Then powder them very fine; after
that slice in your opium, grind them to a powder, and then mix the other powders
with these. Dose from forty to sixty or seventy grains in a glass of white wine Posset*
going to bed; covering up warm and drinking a quart or three pints of the Posset—
Drink while sweating.

* Posset = An old-fashioned remedy for colds consisting of hot milk to which was added
various ingredients, often alcoholic, which made the milk curdle.

*Woodes Rogers. Died in 1732; the date of his birth is unknown. Sea captain, and later Governor
of the Bahamas.*
Daniel Defoe, 1661–1731. Prolific novelist. He wrote Robinson Crusoe *when he was nearly 60
years of age.*

The story of Thomas Dover reads like one of Smollett's novels, but he was no mere swash-buckler, and it was not entirely due to his gift for self-advertisement that his fame as a physician spread throughout Europe. His powder, still essentially of the same composition, maintains its place in the pharmacopoeia of nearly every country in the world; but it will be for future historians to decide who is the more worthy of immortality, the physician who gave us the powder or the pirate who gave us *Robinson Crusoe*.

A few months before he died Thomas Dover retired to his country seat, Stanway House, near the place of his birth in the Cotswold Hills.

Tobias Smollett, 1721–1771. British novelist whose main themes are the depiction of wandering rogues and low life in London.

DUPUYTREN'S CONTRACTURE

BARON GUILLAUME DUPUYTREN 1777–1835

Dupuytren's rise from poverty to be the leading surgeon of France, a baron of the Empire and a millionaire is an enthralling story.

Guillaume Dupuytren was born at Pierre-Buffière, a small town in central France, the son of an advocate of very limited means. So attractive was he as a small boy that a rich lady of Toulouse is said to have kidnapped him. He was, however, restored to his family, and was taken to Paris to be educated at the cost of a cavalry officer who had taken a fancy to him.

His early struggles in Paris as a medical student were almost unbelievably hard. At one time he lived for six weeks on bread and cheese, and was forced to use the fat of the subjects in the dissecting room to make oil for his lamp. His determination to surmount all obstacles won through. In 1802, at the age of 25, he was elected to the surgical staff of the Hôtel Dieu, and in the following year his small book *Propositions sur quelques points d'anatomie* was published. Eleven years later he was appointed surgeon-in-chief, that high office with its unrivalled opportunities for operating and for teaching upon which he had set his heart.

At this venerable hospital Dupuytren toiled for over 30 years. His energy was superabundant; he would pay his first visit to the hospital at six in the morning, and a second at seven in the evening to see the patients upon whom he had operated that day and others whose condition was giving rise to anxiety. He was a wonderful clinical teacher and his lectures kept countless audiences spellbound. At the same time his consulting practice became immense, and it is said that he saw about 10,000 private patients annually.

As an operator he had the utmost self-control, and in an emergency it was said of him, 'Dupuytren was more than a man, he was the god of surgery.' Dupuytren was the first to excise the lower jaw and the first to amputate the cervix of the uterus for carcinoma. Among his greatest triumphs was his operation for the establishment of an artificial anus (lumbar colostomy) and his successful ligation of the subclavian artery. He introduced a new classification of burns, describing six degrees of severity. Today his name lives because he described idiopathic contracture of the palmar fascia, still known throughout the world as Dupuytren's contracture.

This is a common condition in the elderly and is much commoner in men than in women. There is fibrosis of the palmar aponeurosis,

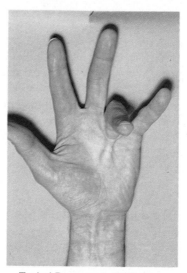

Typical Dupuytren's Contracture

which produces a flexion deformity of the finger at the metacarpo-phalangeal and proximal inter-phalangeal joints, usually starting at the fourth digit and spreading to the fifth and sometimes to the third finger. Since the aponeurosis only extends distally to the base of the middle phalanx, the distal inter-phalangeal joint escapes. The contracture is often bilateral and may occasionally affect the plantar fascia also. The cause of this condition remains as much a mystery today as it was when first described by Dupuytren.

Dupuytren, like so many who have risen from poverty to affluence, was parsimonious, cold and overbearing. He tolerated no rivals, and was called by his contemporaries 'The first of surgeons and the least of men,' and 'The brigand of the Hôtel Dieu.' At the

Hôtel Dieu. Frontage on the Seine, with the towers of Notre Dame in the background

same time all were forced to admit his pre-eminent abilities. The supreme self-confidence of this Surgeon-in-Chief can be summarised in his own words: 'I have been mistaken, but I have been mistaken less than other surgeons.'

One day in November, 1833, while walking to the Hôtel Dieu, Dupuytren suffered a stroke. He was obliged to give up work, although he protested that 'rest is death.' He died on 8th February, 1835, at the age of 57, having 'lifted himself from the most humble to the highest rank, and added another name to the glories of France.'

ERB'S PALSY

WILHELM
HEINRICH
ERB
1840–1921

Wilhelm Erb, the leading German neurologist of his day, was born at Winnweiler, in Bavaria, in 1840, the son of a forester. He began his medical studies at the University of Heidelberg, continued them in Erlangen, and received his Doctor's degree at Munich in 1864.

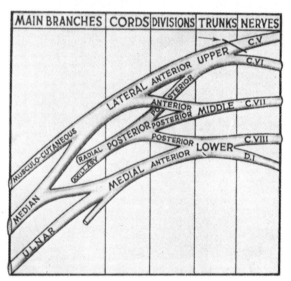

The brachial plexus showing the lesion in Erb's Palsy (arrowed)

After a short period spent in the study of pathology, he returned to Heidelberg as a teacher of medicine and built up a reputation as an original worker and writer.

In 1880 he was appointed Professor of Medicine at Leipzig, but after three years returned to occupy the corresponding position at his old University at Heidelberg. Here he remained, in spite of many tempting calls to other universities, and carried out the important researches which made him world famous.

In 1886 Erb introduced the method of electrodiagnosis by galvanic and induction currents, and he was a pioneer in the field of electrotherapy. Among the most important of his publications were his handbooks on diseases of nerves, the spinal cord and muscular disorders. It was he who coined the term 'tendon reflex.'

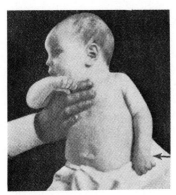

Erb's Palsy. The hand is held in what
is known as the 'policeman's tip'
position

In 1874 Erb described the form of injury to the upper brachial plexus involving the roots of C5 and C6, known as 'Erb's paralysis.' This occurs not uncommonly during childbirth when, as a result of difficult labour, the infant's head becomes displaced excessively, or the shoulder is forcibly depressed. Much more rarely it occurs in adolescent or adult life from a weight falling upon the shoulder, or from other accidental violence.

In a classical paper entitled *Concerning an unusual localisation of brachial plexus paralyses* he described four examples in adult patients and, in addition, wrote 'I have myself observed a case in an infant which had been delivered two months before after a version and subsequent extraction. I found the arm rather mobile, flaccid, and lay extended by the side of the trunk, in a position of full internal rotation, the wrist and fingers were flexed and moved little. More precise observation, which is so difficult in infants, showed complete paralysis of the deltoid, biceps, brachialis and possibly of brachio-radialis . . . There was marked weakness of all the muscles innervated by the radial nerve.' The fact that these cases had a similar neurological deficit led him to state 'It is probable that the lesion in the cases mentioned was localised to the fifth or sixth cervical roots or their anterior branches or at the junction of them both'.

Erb's researches on syphilis of the nervous system and on the muscular dystrophies were also of outstanding importance. In 1878 he clarified the methods of diagnosis of myasthenia gravis.

A great investigator, he was even greater as a clinical teacher and diagnostician. He lived only for science, and when he returned from his very rare vacations invariably brought back the manuscript of some important new work. He was a hard taskmaster, and although everyone respected him, his gruff manner made him feared. Like most Germans, he was passionately fond of music, and he was at a concert when a cerebral haemorrhage occurred and brought a calm and peaceful end. He was then in his eighty-first year.

ESMARCH'S
BANDAGE

FRIEDRICH
VON ESMARCH
1823–1908

Johann Friedrich August von Esmarch was born at Tönning in
Schleswig-Holstein in Germany, just south of the Danish border.
He studied medicine at the Universities of Kiel and Göttingen, and
qualified in 1848.

It was in this year that war between Denmark and Germany
broke out and Esmarch was called up as a military surgeon; during

Esmarch's Bandage applied. All the venous blood is driven from the limb
before the femoral artery is compressed

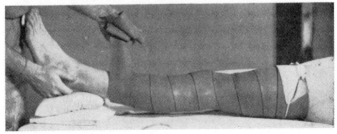

Commencing below, the bandage is unwrapped, leaving only the
first two turns encircling the thigh

65

the campaign he was taken prisoner by the Danes. After the war had ended he returned to Kiel and renewed his association with the university, where three or four years later he was elected professor of clinical surgery.

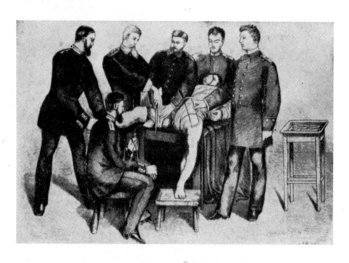

Two illustrations from Esmarch's *Surgeon's Handbook on the Treatment of Wounded in War,* 1878

An ardent supporter of antiseptic surgery, his great interest lay in the treatment of the wounded on the battlefield. To lessen the horrors of warfare became Esmarch's chief mission in life. As a result of the experience he gained in the Danish war, he wrote a book on *Bullet Wounds.*

He saw further active service during the war against Austria in

1866 and yet again in 1870 in the war against France, when he held the rank of Surgeon-General.

Esmarch showed by his writings the necessity of first aid on the battlefield; he advised that every soldier should carry a first-aid outfit, and should be instructed how to use it. A civilian association of trained first-aid workers was organised by him. His *First Aid to the Injured*, published in 1875, became the best-known book on the subject and was translated into English. There is no doubt that Esmarch greatly advanced the surgery of warfare of the 19th century—so much so that he has been called the 'Ambroise Paré of Germany'.

Esmarch's name is perpetuated by his rubber bandage, which, when properly applied, allowed operations to be carried out on the lower extremity, such as removal of a semilunar cartilage of the knee-joint, through a bloodless field.

Soon after his return from the Danish war Esmarch married the daughter of his teacher, Stromeyer, who was then professor at Kiel. By his second marriage in 1872 to Princess Henriette von Schleswig-Holstein he became an uncle of Emperor William II, the notorious 'Kaiser Bill' of World War I.

In Germany Esmarch enjoyed the highest reputation as a surgeon and a teacher. In his native town of Tönning there is a statue erected to him. When he retired from the chair in 1899 Emperor William conferred upon him the title of 'Excellency.'

He died at the age of 85.

George Friedrich Louis Stromeyer, 1804–1876. Professor of Surgery, Kiel, was the Father of Military Surgery in Germany.

Ambroise Paré, 1510–1590, the great French military surgeon, discarded the use of boiling oil to staunch haemorrhage after amputation of a limb, and re-introduced the use of a ligature and dry dressings. One of his most famous sayings was 'Je l'ay pansay: Dieu l'a guerit' (I dressed him and God healed him).

THE FALLOPIAN TUBES

GABRIEL FALLOPIUS 1523–1562

Gabriel Fallopius was one of the most illustrious anatomists of the sixteenth century. In the course of a brief career (he died when he was 39 years of age) he made a number of discoveries.

Fallopius gave a good description of the human oviducts, which have been known ever since as the Fallopian Tubes. He described the ovaries and the round ligaments, and he gave the names that they now bear to the vagina and the placenta. He discovered the semi-circular canals and was the first to describe the trigeminal, auditory and glossopharyngeal nerves.

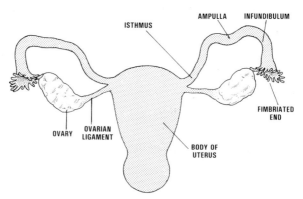

The Fallopian tubes and adjacent structures

Fallopius was the favourite pupil of the great anatomist Vesalius. It was Vesalius and some of his contemporaries of the Italian school who founded the modern science of anatomy.

It must be explained that it was not until the sixteenth century that men commenced to dissect the human body systematically and to record by means of the written word, as well as by illustration, the complex disposition and pathways of the structures they unravelled. Owing to religious scruples concerning human dissection, from the second to the sixteenth centuries there was absolutely

Vesalius demonstrating Anatomy at Padua in 1546. In 1551
Fallopius succeeded his master
From the painting by E. J. C. Hamman in the Musée des Beaux-Arts, Marseilles

no advance in anatomical knowledge. The brilliant exception was Mondino de Luzzi (1270?–1326) of Bologna who in 1316 wrote the first anatomical textbook worthy of the name. The works of Galen, and of Galen only, were accepted as the alpha and omega of anatomical learning. What Galen had decreed was not only the final authority, but anyone who questioned that authority ran risks similar to those encountered by the bold spirits who dared to assert that the earth was not flat. On the rare occasions when anatomical courses were given at the universities, menials performed the

Andreas Vesalius, 1514–1564, performed dissections successively in Bologna, Pisa, Basle and Padua. His great work De Humani Corporis Fabrica was published in Basle in 1543.

dissections while the Professor read what Galen had to say on the subject. So rolled by, not years, but centuries of the perpetration and perpetuation of the grossest errors so far as the study of anatomy was concerned. At long last all this was changed by Vesalius and his pupils.

Gabriel Fallopius was born at Modena in North Italy. He held an ecclesiastical appointment in the cathedral of his native town, but he gave this up in order to study medicine. Fallopius had the greatest respect for his master, Vesalius, and in 1551 the pupil succeeded the teacher as Professor of Anatomy in the University of Padua.

Fallopius was very versatile. Besides his anatomical work he taught and wrote on chemistry, botany and surgery. He had charge of the botanical garden at Padua and was a good practical surgeon. His name will never be forgotten.

FERGUSSON'S LION FORCEPS
FERGUSSON'S MOUTH GAG
FERGUSSON'S SPECULUM

SIR WILLIAM FERGUSSON 1808–1877

Sir William Fergusson was the greatest surgeon of his day, indeed he was probably the greatest of the pre-Listerian operators. It is remarkable that between 1828 and 1864 (before the days of anaesthesia and asepsis) Fergusson was able to claim 129 successes

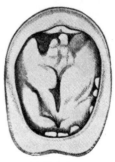
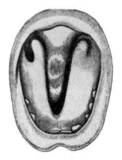

(A) Cleft Palate	(B) The same fourteen days after operation

(Woodcut from Sir William Fergusson's Lectures published in 1872)

out of 134 cases of cleft palate upon which he operated, and among 400 cases of hare-lip operated upon by him during the same period there were only three failures. His speed at amputation through the thigh was prodigious.

'Supposing I had to have my leg amputated—who is the best man to do it?' enquired H.R.H. Albert the Prince Consort in 1849 of one of the Court officials. 'Why, Fergusson, by all means,' was the answer. 'Then,' replied the Prince, 'he shall be my surgeon.'

William Fergusson, the son of the Laird of Lochmaben, Dumfriesshire, was born at Prestonpans, Scotland, and was educated at the High School, Edinburgh, and later went on to the University in that city. Originally he intended to follow the law, but finding the lawyer's office most uncongenial, he abandoned it for the study of medicine. At the age of 17 he became a pupil of Robert Knox. Under Knox's tuition he became a first-class dissector. It was this training in anatomy which doubtless stood him in such stead in the practice of surgery.

King's College Hospital in 1845

In 1829, at the age of 21, Fergusson was admitted to the Fellowship of the Royal College of Surgeons of Edinburgh, having qualified L.R.C.S. one year previously. Two years later he became Surgeon to the Dispensary. It was while holding this office that he tied the subclavian artery, an operation that had been performed only twice before in Scotland. At the age of 25 he married an heiress, and six years later he was appointed Surgeon to the Royal Infirmary in succession to Robert Liston, and so successful was he that his practice rivalled that of Professor Syme. In 1840 he was

Robert Knox, 1791–1862. M.D. (Edin.). Lecturer in Anatomy. After the Burke and Hare incident the school declined, and he was forced to seek other posts.
Robert Liston (see p. 145).
James Syme (see p. 215).

offered the vacant Chair of Surgery at King's College, London, and Fergusson, always a man of energy and enterprise, migrated from Edinburgh to London. It was not long before he was elected a Fellow of the Royal College of Surgeons of England. Fergusson was tall, dignified, with handsome features, large dark eyes and a benevolent expression. His hands were large and powerful.

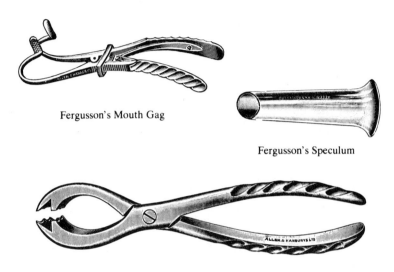

Fergusson's Mouth Gag

Fergusson's Speculum

Fergusson's Lion Forceps

Fergusson invented many instruments, some of which are in use to-day. His lion forceps for excision of the upper jaw, his mouth gag and his vaginal speculum are the best known. It was he who coined the term 'conservative surgery,' and in suitable cases he excised a diseased joint instead of sacrificing the limb. Among his many surgical accomplishments was that of cutting for stone in the bladder, which he performed so quickly that it was said that if one blinked one might see no operation at all. During all his operations he expected absolute silence; he himself never spoke until the patient was off the operating table. In 1855 he was appointed Surgeon Extraordinary to Queen Victoria, in 1866 a baronetcy was conferred upon him and in 1870 he served as President of the Royal College of Surgeons of England. He died from Bright's disease at the age of 69, but he was performing operations before large numbers of spectators a few weeks prior to his death. He was buried at West Linton, near his beloved Scottish home. Sir James Paget described Fergusson as 'the greatest master of the surgical art, and the greatest practical surgeon of our time.'

Sir James Paget (see p. 179).

THE VEINS
OF GALEN
(The Internal Cerebral Veins)

GALEN
A.D. 130–200

After Hippocrates the name of Galen is the greatest in ancient medicine. Born at Pergamum in Asia Minor (now Bergama, in Turkey) in A.D. 130, he was the son of an architect. Galen studied at the best medical schools of the day, including Smyrna, Corinth and Alexandria. Returning to his native city in his twenty-eighth year, he remained at Pergamum for four years, during which time he held the post of surgeon to the gladiators.

At the age of 32 he journeyed to Rome and there commenced to practise. He gave public lectures on anatomy and soon became a fashionable physician. His popularity grew; he was summoned to treat Marcus Aurelius, who, after a heavy meal of cheese, had developed intestinal colic. The patient recovered quickly, and so impressed was the Emperor that he made Galen his personal physician. Galen accompanied his imperial master on an expedition to Germany. After the death of Marcus Aurelius, Galen was appointed physician successively to the Emperors Commodus and Septimus Severus. Having occupied the position of the foremost physician in Rome for several years, Galen withdrew from practice in that city to devote his life to study, travel, teaching and writing. He became the most voluminous writer, not only among the ancient physicians, but among all the ancient philosophers.

He was the first experimental physiologist: it was he who first proved that arteries contain and carry blood. Although his writings contained many errors, they constituted the only available source of information on medical subjects for centuries. Galen was the first to describe the cranial nerves and the sympathetic system: he made the first experimental bisection of the spinal cord, and proved that it caused paraplegia: he formulated the first valid explanation

75

of the mechanism of respiration: he chronicled the signs of inflammation* even as they are taught today: he differentiated pneumonia from pleurisy: he was the first to describe an arterial aneurysm.

Galen had great faith in drugs and collected plants from all parts of the known world. He is said to have owned a shop for the sale of drugs near the Forum, in Rome.

Galen does not set forth many clinical accounts of cases, but he does not omit to record several extraordinary cures. His greatest labours were in anatomy and physiology. He does not appear to have had the opportunity of dissecting the human body; most of his anatomical knowledge was founded on the dissection of pigs and apes. It is strange that the Romans, who delighted in blood and slaughter, recoiled in horror from the idea of opening a dead body.

Galen regarded himself as a disciple of Hippocrates, but he had not the simplicity and genius of the Father of Medicine. Hippocrates could say 'I do not know.' Galen had an answer to every problem, and his answer was accepted not only by his contemporaries, but by posterity for no less than 15 centuries. No other physician has ever had such influence; as time went on he was regarded as almost infallible. As late as the year 1559 John Geynes, M.D. Oxford, was summoned before the Royal College of Physicians of London for casting doubt on the infallibility of Galen, and he only saved himself from professional degradation by publicly acknowledging his error.

Nothing can detract from Galen's place in the history of medicine. He represents the culmination of the study of the healing art by the Greeks, and was, indeed, a Prince of Physicians. Of the books Galen wrote, about 80 are still in existence; most of them are on medicine, but some are on natural science and logic.

---

* Redness, heat, pain, swelling and loss of function. The first four were recorded by Celsus. Galen himself added only the last.

Aulus Aurelius Cornelius Celsus, circa 25 A.D. *Roman encyclopaedist and medical author.*

GAMGEE
TISSUE

JOSEPH
SAMPSON
GAMGEE
1828-1886

On 18th February, 1880, Mr. Sampson Gamgee, Surgeon to the Queen's Hospital at Birmingham, gave a clinical lecture entitled *On Absorbent and Antiseptic Surgical Dressings.* It was in the nature of a demonstration, and the scene may be reconstructed somewhat as follows:

'Here,' said the lecturer, 'is a piece of finest cotton-wool. You see, it floats on water, and will continue to float for weeks. Now into this tumbler of water I drop a pledget of cotton-wool made absorbent by the removal of oily matter, and you see that it sinks to the bottom in a very few seconds ... Here again is a piece of ordinary calico bandage. It floats in the basin like a plank on a pond. Now here is a piece of absorbent open woven bandage, and you see that it sinks the instant I drop it on to the water.

'Clinical experience has demonstrated the great value of absorbent materials. Discharges drain through them so rapidly that wounds are kept clean and the surrounding parts dry.'

In this way Gamgee demonstrated the principle of his absorbent dressing, which has been named after him. Gamgee Tissue consists of a layer of absorbent cotton-wool between two layers of absorbent gauze, combining the powers both of compression and absorption.

According to Gamgee, the absorbent dressing was the invention of Dr. Mathias Mayor, of Lausanne, but the idea of combining absorbent cotton-wool with compressing gauze was Gamgee's own. It was he who insisted that the material should be manufactured in an antiseptic manner. In his own words, 'The soothing surgical

Mathias Mayor, 1776-1846. Surgeon, Cantonal Hospital, Lausanne, Switzerland.

pressure is like that which you interchange with the hand of a lady. Your hand adapts itself to hers, and gently presses it wherever it can touch it, but nowhere squeezes it for fear of offending.'

Joseph Sampson Gamgee was the eldest son of a veterinary surgeon. He was born at Leghorn, Italy. In 1847 he went to London and entered the Royal Veterinary College as a student. He obtained

The Queen's Hospital, Birmingham, 1841

his veterinary diploma, but then went to University College, where he had a brilliant career as a medical student, winning many prizes. He became a member of the Royal College of Surgeons of England in 1854, and in 1855 was appointed Surgeon to the British Italian Legion. During the Crimean war he was placed in charge of the Legion Hospital at Malta, and gained experience among the wounded evacuated to that island. In 1857 he was appointed Surgeon to the Queen's Hospital, Birmingham, and became one of the leading surgeons of that city. He died in 1886.

GLAUBER'S SALTS

JOHANN RUDOLF
GLAUBER
1603–1668

Glauber might, with justice, be designated the first manufacturing pharmaceutical chemist. His considerable activities extended also far into the realms of commercial and industrial chemistry.

Johann Glauber was born at Carlstadt in Bavaria in 1603. He 'never frequented the universities, nor even had a mind to do so,' and it was his opinion that had he had a university education he would never have arrived at 'that knowledge of Nature that I now possess.'

Nothing is known of his parents, but they must have been fairly well-to-do, for as a young man he set out on the Grand Tour. Tarrying at Vienna, he was stricken with 'the Hungarian disease' (gastroenteritis), and were it not for this misfortune it is unlikely that his name would have become notable to the medical profession. The incident that changed the course of his life is best described in his own words:

> On the advice of friends I dragged myself to a certain spring situated about a league from Neustadt. I had brought with me a loaf of bread, but with no hope of being able to eat it. Arrived at the spring I took the loaf from my pocket and made a hole in it so that I could use it as a cup. As I drank the water my appetite returned, and I ended by eating the improvised cup in its turn. I made several visits to the spring and was soon miraculously cured of my illness.

The marvellous salt contained in this spring water (later identified as sodium sulphate) so impressed Glauber that he determined to commercialise it. On returning home he satisfied himself that this salt was the same as that which he obtained from the residue after distilling a mixture of sea-water and vitriol (sulphuric acid). He named this salt *Sal mirabile Glauber*. By no means was this all that accrued from this experiment. The distillate he found to be spirits of salt (hydrochloric acid) and he was the first to manufacture hydrochloric acid on a large scale. The latter was probably his principal contribution to the development of chemistry, while the former made him far-famed as a pharmacist. While carrying on this business he lived successively in Salzburg, Kissingen, Frankfurt-on-the-Main and Cologne, before finally he decided to make his permanent home in Amsterdam. In spite of the success of his project, he was always experimenting, and he was the first chemist to prepare a large number of chemical substances, including various salts of antimony, zinc and tin. He distilled ammonia from bones, and made sal ammoniac by the addition of sea-water. He also produced sulphate of ammonia for use as a fertiliser, and it is used in this connexion today; for long this fertiliser was known by the name given to it by Glauber—*Sal Ammoniacum Secretum Glauberi.*

Glauber, always anxious to turn his knowledge to practical account, acted in the capacity of a consulting industrial chemist, in this rôle he added considerably to the knowledge of the chemistry of the wine and spirit industry, and also to the manufacture of dyestuffs.

One secret that he claimed to have discovered he would neither sell nor publish— it was that of the *alkahest*, or universal solvent. To make this known, he pleaded, 'would encourage luxury and Godlessness.'

Unmitigated success made Glauber extremely unpopular with his rivals. Undoubtedly he suffered much, not only on this account, but because many of the fruits of his labour were stolen and claimed by others as their own inventions.

He seems to have borne these tribulations stoically and without rancour, for he writes:

'I grieve over the ignorance of my contemporaries and the ingratitude of man. I fulfil my career, and await my reward.'

Glauber was the author of some 30 books. He died at his home in Amsterdam in 1668. After his death, for about 100 years his name was revered by the pharmacists of Europe, and the sign of their calling was a gilded wooden bust of Glauber's head placed over the entrance of their shops. Perhaps this was the reward that Glauber awaited.

THE GRAAFIAN FOLLICLE

REGNIER DE GRAAF
1641–1673

Regnier de Graaf was born at Schoonhaven, in the Netherlands, the son of Cornelius de Graaf, a celebrated architect and inventor of hydraulic machines. When the time arrived, young de Graaf decided on a medical career, and enrolled as a student at Utrecht. After a short period he transferred to the University of Leyden, which at that time was one of the foremost medical centres in Europe. Here he sat at the feet of that famous anatomist Sylvius de la Boe, and, incidentally, among his fellow students was Niels Stensen.

Inspired by his teacher Sylvius, de Graaf carried out a series of experiments on the physiology of the pancreas. He constructed an external pancreatic fistula in a dog, employing a goose-quill. His conclusions respecting the nature of the juice were largely erroneous, but they gained for him the M.D. Leyden at the age of 22 years, and his findings formed the basis of knowledge on the function of the pancreas for 200 years, until the French physiologist Claude Bernard shattered them.

In 1665 de Graaf went to Paris where he was well received in scientific circles, and where he arranged for the publication of a French edition of his M.D. thesis. He travelled through France, studying anatomy and making many dissections. In 1666 he returned to Holland and practised for a time at Delft. In 1668 he published

Francois Sylvius de la Boe, 1614–1672. Professor of Practical Medicine, Leyden, Holland. Described the aqueduct of Sylvius.
Claude Bernard, 1813–1878. Professor of Medicine and Physiology, Paris. Came to Paris as a hopeful dramatist, and remained to become the master physiologist of his time.

a treatise on the male organs of generation, which contains an excellent account of the structure of the testis. Later, while in practice, he invented a syringe for injecting the arteries of the cadaver, and a little later adapted this syringe for use in the administration of clysters (enemas), which were then enjoying unbridled popularity throughout Europe.

In 1672, while still in practice as a physician, de Graaf published his greatest work—that on the female generative organs. In this book the opinions of both ancients and moderns are assessed

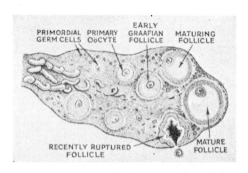

critically and tested by comparison with the author's own dissections. In 1667 Stensen, the famous Danish anatomist, had stated that the so-called female testes of the older anatomists were not testes at all, but egg-producing organs corresponding with those of birds and other egg-laying creatures. It was Stensen who coined the term ovary, and maintained that even female mammals ovulated. It was de Graaf who proved this theory by discovering the Graafian follicles of the ovaries and by describing their maturation. 'These little vesicles,' he said, 'perfectly resemble the eggs contained in the ovaries of birds.'

By dissecting rabbits at varying intervals after coitus, de Graaf discovered the corpus luteum, and he traced the passage of the ova down the oviducts to the uterus. De Graaf based these epoch-making discoveries on experiments performed on more than a hundred rabbits, and forty goats, cows, dogs, cats and other animals.

His book was accepted in his day and generation throughout the seats of learning in Europe, and it would seem that he should have been awarded an academic post, for which he yearned and which he merited—but not so. In 1672 the chair of anatomy at Leyden became vacant by the death of his master Sylvius, but de Graaf was not appointed, apparently because he was a Catholic. In 1673 he sent to the Royal Society of London the first letters of his townsman, Anthony van Leeuwenhoek, the inventor of the microscope.

De Graaf died of the plague in his thirty-second year.

Antonj van Leeuwenhoek. See footnote, p. 161.

GRAM'S STAIN

CHRISTIAN
GRAM
1853–1938

It is interesting to know that the discoverer of Gram's method of staining bacteria, known to every final-year medical student and every doctor in all corners of the Earth, was not a professional bacteriologist, but a physician and a teacher of general medicine.

Christian Gram was born in Copenhagen, the son of Julius Gram, LL.D., Professor of Common Law in the university of that city. In 1871, at the age of 18, Christian enrolled at the University of Copenhagen to study botany, and he pursued his botanical studies for three years before becoming a medical student. Throughout his life he cherished a love for, and knowledge of, plants; this knowledge formed the basis of his pharmacological interest, and his botanical training made him extremely familiar with the use of the microscope.

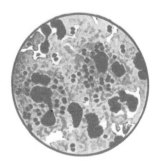

Gonococci (Gram's stain)

Gram graduated M.B. Copenhagen in 1878, and in 1882 he took the M.D. degree and gained the University medal with a thesis *On the Size of the Red Blood Corpuscles in Man.*

In this thesis he described the method of drawing blood into a

84

capillary tube, sealing the ends of the tube, allowing the blood to clot, breaking the tube at the border of the clot and the serum, blowing out the serum on to a glass slide, and examining the erythrocytes. His measurements were of great exactitude, and are quoted to the present day. He also called attention to the increase in size of the erythrocytes in jaundice and in pernicious anaemia (macrocytes).

From 1883 to 1885 Gram studied bacteriology and pharmacology at various German universities, publishing as a short paper in *Friedländer's Journal* his observations on a new differential staining method of bacteria (Gram stain). An unconfirmed tradition has it that this discovery was the result of an accident—Lugol's solution

The Old Royal Frederik's Hospital*

being upset over a freshly stained bacterial smear with subsequent attempts to wash the iodine off with alcohol. This, if true, only goes to show that an epoch-making discovery is sometimes made by

* It was through the iron railing of this hospital that the medical student wearing the 'Goloshes of Happiness' (but ignorant of their power) became entrapped with his head out and his body inside. Hans Andersen's Fairy Tales.

Hans Christian Andersen, 1805–1875. The most gifted writer of fairy tales that the world has known.

Jean Guillaume Auguste Lugol (see p. 152).

taking advantage of a fortuitous happening. The discovery which has perpetuated Gram's name was made while he was pursuing post-graduate studies in Berlin. Later the author of a German textbook on bacteriology annexed this discovery for glory of the Fatherland by the ingenious claim 'The Gram stain, which Christian Gram in 1884 discovered at Berlin.' As Gram described in his paper 'many cocci, particularly pneumococci and the cocci found in pyaemia, are stained intensely, whilst some few other bacteria, such as typhoid, are decolorized,' to which the editor of the journal (Carl Friedländer), quite contrary to what was the general custom, wisely and generously added a footnote, 'Undoubtedly posterity will be able to verify this.'

Gram's stain (notice that this should be spelt with a capital G), enables us to classify bacteria into two large sub-divisions, the Gram positive and Gram negative organisms. The former include the Clostridia, Staphylococci and Streptococci while examples of the latter are Salmonella, Shigella, Pseudomanas, Escherichia, Proteus, Klebsiella and Bacteroides.

On returning to Copenhagen, Gram became resident physician at the Kommunehospitalet, and for some years district physician in Copenhagen. In 1891 he was appointed Lecturer in Pharmacology, and later in the same year Professor of Pharmacology. In 1892 he became Physician-in-Chief at the Royal Frederik's Hospital.* In 1900 he changed his Professorship of Pharmacology for that of Medicine. Gram's public and teaching duties did not leave him much time for scientific work, and his later publications were mainly clinical; he published altogether four volumes of clinical lectures.

Professor Gram enjoyed a very large private practice, but he never allowed this to interfere with his hospital duties; each single patient in his department was seen and examined by himself with thoroughness and exactitude. Professor Gram was much loved by his patients, and to his pupils he was at the same time an authoritative teacher and a good friend.

After his retirement, Professor Gram spent the last 15 years of his life in pursuit of his first love—botany, and interested himself

---

* The Royal Frederik's Hospital, built in 1757, is now the Museum for Applied Art. In 1910 the Royal Frederik's Hospital was replaced by the modern Rigshospitalet, erected further from the City centre.

Carl Friedländer, 1847–1887. Pathologist, Friedrichshain Hospital, Berlin.

in measures for preventing tuberculosis. Doubtless he felt the latter was his impelling duty, because he had lost his wife from pulmonary tuberculosis.

.

GRAVES' DISEASE

ROBERT JAMES GRAVES 1796–1853

As in descriptive anatomy, so in clinical medicine, surgery and pathology there are those who strive to do away with proper names, and employ a purely anatomico-pathological nomenclature. There is much to be said for this method of classification, although it is

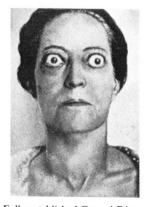

Fully established Graves' Disease

sad that in many instances the discoverer's name becomes lost to the majority of the profession. In the case of Graves' disease there was an additional incentive to change the appellation, seeing that it is quite certain that Graves was not the first to describe the condition known by his name.

The first attempt in this direction—and for a time it was very successful—was to call the condition exophthalmic goitre. In due course it was pointed out by high authorities that some patients with this condition had no exophthalmos, while a few others had no goitre.

It was then agreed to recommend the use of the term primary toxic goitre, and this is widely employed, in spite of the fact that in a few cases there is no goitre. For these reasons George Crile, Jnr., admitted 'Because of the difficulties in terminology, I am forced to fall back on the term "Graves' disease",' and, like Crile, more and more authors in the British Commonwealth and the U.S.A. are once again employing the term 'Graves' disease.' On the Continent the disease is known as Basedow's Disease).

Robert Graves was the third son of Dr. Richard Graves, Dean of Armagh, and was born in 1796. After a brilliant student career at Trinity College, Dublin, he spent three years travelling. He had a great facility for learning languages and spoke German so perfectly

The Meath Hospital in Graves' day

that he was taken for a German spy in Austria and was imprisoned for 10 days.

On returning to Dublin, Graves put up his plate as a physician, and soon afterwards was elected physician to the Meath Hospital. It was here that he introduced, against much opposition, the system of clinical teaching whereby the student actually examined the patient as well as writing the clinical history. This system, which emanated from Paris, was not adopted by the English and Scottish medical schools until much later, and was largely responsible for making the Dublin School of Medicine famous throughout Europe.

Karl Adolph Basedow, 1799–1854. General practitioner, Mersburg, Germany.
George Crile, Jnr. Contemporary. Chief Surgeon, Cleveland, Clinic, Cleveland, Ohio, U.S.A.
*   Has carried on his father's famous thyroid clinic.*

'Walking the Wards' by medical students was first introduced in England by Sir William Blízard, F.R.S., 1743–1836, Surgeon to the London Hospital.

When he was 39 years of age Graves published an excellent account of the disease which bears his name, and it was the lucidity, rather than the originality, of this monograph that attracted so much attention. He wrote: 'I have lately seen three cases of violent and long continued palpitations in females, in each of which the same peculiarity presented itself, viz: enlargement of the thyroid gland; the size of this gland, at all times considerably greater than natural . . . It was observed that the eyes assumed a singular appearance, for the eyeballs were apparently enlarged, so that when she slept or tried to shut her eyes, the lids were incapable of closing. When the eyes were open, the white sclerotic could be seen, to a breadth of several lines, all around the cornea.'

Tall, dark and distinguished, Graves' very presence, as well as his fluent delivery, enhanced his admirable clinical teaching, which is summarised in his *Clinical Lectures* (1848). Perhaps Graves' most important contribution to clinical medicine was his insistence that the pulse must be timed by the watch. In his own opinion the greatest advance that he effected was the abandonment of bleeding and starving of patients with pyrexia, and he requested that his epitaph should read 'He fed fevers.'

GRAWITZ TUMOUR OF THE KIDNEY

PAUL
GRAWITZ
1850–1932

Paul Grawitz was born at Zerrin bei Bütow, situated in Pomerania on the shores of the Baltic Sea. He studied medicine at the Universities of Berlin and Halle, and qualified in 1873. After qualification he became an assistant at the Pathological Institute at

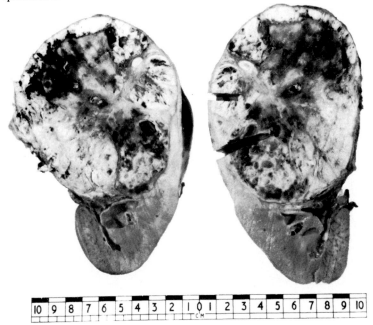

A Grawitz tumour (clear cell carcinoma) of the kidney.

Berlin, where he worked under the world-famous Professor Virchow. So engrossed did he become in the study of pathology that he determined to make this branch his career. He continued to work under Virchow for 10 years.

Grawitz is known today by his work on neoplasms of the kidney. Grawitz tumour, a renal adenocarcinoma, is the most common new growth of the kidney. The tumour often occupies one or other pole of the kidney, the seat of election being the upper pole. This fact, and the colour of the tumour (characteristically it is butter-yellow, due to contained lipoid) led to the erroneous belief that the neoplasm was derived from misplaced adrenal tissue, and for many years it was called a hypernephroma. The latter inaccurate term still lingers. Microscopically, the tumour cells are typically large with an abundant foamy cytoplasm and a small central densely staining nucleus ('clear cell tumour'). Typically spread occurs by the blood stream with growth along the renal vein into the inferior vena cava. Deposits in the lung, bones and brain are common. Occasionally a solitary blood-borne deposit occurs, so that removal of the primary growth together with this deposit has been followed by prolonged survival. Grawitz published the first thorough study of these neoplasms in 1884.

The Pathological Institute, Greifswald, where Grawitz worked for 37 years

Rudolf Virchow, 1821–1902. Director of the Pathological Institute of the Charité Hospital, Berlin.

Shortly after this, and probably as a result of this brilliant piece of work, Grawitz was called to the Chair of Pathology in the University of Greifswald, a post that he held for 37 years.

In the course of his long career Grawitz made many important contributions to pathology. In his latter years he was much occupied with researches in tissue culture. One of his greatest interests in life was the pathological museum at Greifswald. He spent two hours daily in its care, mounting specimens and writing descriptions of them. Grawitz died in his eighty-second year, having made the University of Greifswald famous (Greifswald is a town of 40,000 inhabitants situated on the Baltic coast of North East Germany).

HEBERDEN'S NODES

WILLIAM
HEBERDEN
1710–1801

Heberden's description of his nodes is as follows:

Digitorum Nodi. What are these little hard knobs, about the size of a small pea, which are frequently seen upon the fingers, particularly a little below the top, near the joint? They have no connection with the gout, being found in persons who never had it; they continue for life; and being hardly ever attended by pain, or disposed to become sores, are rather unsightly than inconvenient, though they must be of some little hindrance to the free use of the fingers.

It was these 80 words that perpetuated his name and called into being the Heberden Society for the study of Rheumatic Diseases. It should be noted that Heberden made the significant statement that the nodes were not due to gout. He did not say to what they were due. They are, in fact, associated with osteo-arthrosis, commoner in women than in men.

Heberden's description of his nodes is actually one of his minor achievements, not to be compared in importance with some of his other discoveries. It was Heberden who first recognised angina pectoris, and it was Heberden who first differentiated chickenpox from smallpox.

Born on London in 1710, William Heberden was educated at Cambridge, where he distinguished himself in classics. Having taken his medical degree, he practised in Cambridge for about ten years and gave an annual course of lectures on *materia medica*. In 1748 he migrated to London, becoming a Fellow of the Royal College of Physicians, and commenced practice in the capital. Possessed of considerable experience, wide learning, and culture, he soon established himself. He continued to practise in London for over fifty years and earned a reputation that has not been surpassed by any physician.

Dr. Samuel Johnson, in his last illness, being asked what physician he had summoned, answered 'Dr. Heberden, *ultimus Romanorum*, the last of our learned physicians.'

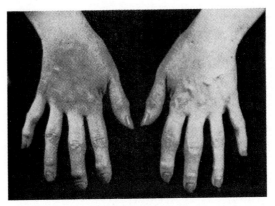

Heberden's Nodes

Dr. Heberden died in 1801, at the great age of 91. in the following year William Heberden the younger, who was himself a distinguished physician, brought out the Latin edition of his father's *Commentaries on the History and Cure of Diseases*, together with an English translation. The Commentaries were built up from notes taken in Latin during more than half a century of busy practice. Heberden's Commentaries are among the greatest monuments of clinical medicine, excelled only by the *Aphorisms* of Hippocrates.

Samuel Johnson, LL.D. (Dublin), 1709–1784. Famous Lexicographer and Writer. His Dictionary appeared in 1755.

HEGAR'S DILATORS
HEGAR'S SIGN

ALFRED
HEGAR
1830–1914

Where dilation of the cervix uteri is performed for a therapeutic purpose, as in dysmenorrhoea, use is made of Hegar's dilators—a series of metal bougies of varying sizes—invented by the eminent German gynaecologist Alfred Hegar.

Hegar has also given his name to a valuable sign for the diagnosis of pregnancy—Hegar's sign. The sign consists in a softening of the

A Hegar's Dilator

uterus, at the isthmus just between the cervix and the body of the organ, between the sixth and twelfth weeks of gestation. The sign was actually described in 1884 by C. Reinl, Hegar's first assistance, but Hegar's name has become attached to it because it was Hegar who made it so widely known. Carl Reinl made no other contribution to gynaecology, neither did he obtain a post of distinction.

Alfred Hegar was born at Darmstadt, where his father was a much respected local medical practitioner. After studying at the universities of Giessen, Heidelberg, Berlin and Vienna, Alfred Hegar obtained his degree in 1852. He practised for some years in his native city of Darmstadt, and in 1864 was called to the chair of Obstetrics and Gynaecology at Freiburg.

Professor Hegar's numerous writings included a manual of operative gynaecology, monographs on retention of the placenta, on oöphorectomy, and on diagnosis of pregnancy. He also wrote a biography of Semmelweis, whose ardent disciple he was; indeed, Hegar was one of the very first to implement the principles of antisepsis.

Hegar was one of the pioneers in Germany of the modern operation of oöphorectomy, introduced by the Englishmen Lawson Tait and Spencer Wells, and he devised a valuable operation for the repair of the perineum. Also he was the first in Germany to perform myomectomy for uterine fibroids.

The University of Freiburg

Hegar was a great operator, writer and teacher, and he enhanced the fame of Freiburg as a centre of gynaecological study and research. In 1889 his colleagues and pupils presented him with a volume of essays especially written to commemorate the 25th anniversary of his professorship. After holding the chair for 30 years he resigned his professorship in 1904, and died at the ripe age of 84 years.

Hegar was always a prodigious worker, and it is said that in summer time he not infrequently began to operate at 5 o'clock in the morning. He enjoyed wonderful health and vigour right to the end of his life.

Ignaz Philipp Semmelweis, 1818–1865. Professor of Obstetrics, Budapest, was the first to attribute the transmission of puerperal sepsis to the hands of those in attendance. This explanation was received with derision, and he was dismissed from his post.

Robert Lawson Tait, 1845–1899. Surgeon, The Womens' Hospital, Birmingham. A great exponent of oöphorectomy and an opponent of antisepsis. He employed soap and water, and was, in truth, the pioneer of asepsis.

THE HIPPOCRATIC FACIES

HIPPOCRATES
(?)460–370 B.C.

By common consent Hippocrates is regarded as the Father of Medicine and the greatest physician of all time. He was the son of a physician and was born about 460 B.C. on the island of Cos, in the Ægean Archipelago.

The true practice of medicine began with Hippocrates: it was he who severed the art of healing from witchcraft and superstition.

Hippocrates led a wandering life, practising and teaching in various parts of Greece. He had many pupils, including his two sons. He and his pupils recorded their observations in writing. These reports of actual cases are model clinical records unsurpassed for nearly two thousand years. Many of the descriptions of diseases such as phthisis, puerperal septicaemia and epilepsy might, with but few changes, take their place in any modern medical text-book.

Perhaps his best-known description is that of the face of a patient suffering from advanced peritonitis, now known as the Hippocratic Facies:

'You should observe thus in acute diseases; first the countenance of the patient, if it be like those of persons in health, and especially if it be like its usual self, for this is best of all. But the opposite are

98

the worst, such as these: a sharp nose, hollow eyes, sunken temples, the ears cold, contracted, and their lobes turned outwards, the skin about the forehead rough, stretched and parched, the colour of the face greenish or livid. If the symptoms do not subside (in a day and a night) be it known for certain that the end is at hand.'

The most famous work of hippocrates is his *Aphorisms*. These contain brief generalisations, based upon his vast experience. The aphorisms of Hipocrates have been revered by clinicians throughout the ages; and many of them have passed into proverbs. To select a few:

Life is short and art is long; the crisis is fleeting, experiment risky, decision difficult.
No head injury is so slight that it should be neglected, or so severe that life should be despaired of.
Convulsions supervening on a wound are deadly. (Tetanus.)
When sleep puts an end to delirium it is a good sign.
Those naturally very fat are more liable to sudden death than the thin.
In jaundice it is a grave matter if the liver become indurated.
Eunuchs do not take the gout, nor become bald.
In acute diseases, coldness of the extremities is bad.

Hippocrates was no specialist; he treated every kind of malady. His treatment was based upon common-sense principles and was largely expectant. Good nursing and a rational diet played a great part.

The medical profession pay homage to Hippocrates by taking the Hippocratic Oath when they enter the portals of medicine as qualified practitioners. The following are excerpts from the Hippocratic Oath:

I swear by Apollo the physician . . . that, according to my ability and judgement, I will keep this oath to reckon him who taught me this Art equally dear to me as my parents . . . I will follow that system of regimen which, according to my ability and judgement, I consider for the benefit of my patients, and abstain from whatever is deleterious and mischievous. I will give no deadly medicine to anyone if asked, nor suggest any such counsel . . . Into whatever houses I enter, I will go into them for the benefit of the sick, and will abstain from every voluntary act of mischief and corruption . . . Whatever in connection with my professional practice I see or hear I will not divulge, as reckoning all such should be kept secret. While I continue to keep this oath unviolated, may it be granted to me to enjoy life and the practice of the Art, respected by all men. But should I trespass and violate this Oath, may the reverse be my lot.

The date of Hippocrates' death is uncertain, but it occurred between 377 and 359 B.C. The latter date would make him 101 years of age at the time of his death. Such longevity is the more remarkable seeing that at that era the average expectation of life was much shorter than it is today.

It is probable that what are now known collectively as the writings of Hippocrates were first brought together in the third century B.C. Manuscript copies of this compilation were circulated widely in Greece and the Middle East, but the *Complete Works* were not printed until 1525, when a Latin version was issued at Rome. The printed Greek text was brought out by the famous Venetian printer Aldus Manutius in 1526. The *Genuine Works of Hippocrates* were translated into English in 1849 by Francis Adams.

Francis Adams, 1796–1861. General Practitioner, Banchory, Kincardine, Scotland. One of the greatest classical scholars the medical profession has produced.

HIRSCHSPRUNG'S DISEASE

HARALD HIRSCHSPRUNG 1830–1916

Congenital dilatation of the colon is known as Hirschsprung's disease, because Professor Harald Hirschsprung, of Copenhagen, gave the first full and convincing account of the condition in 1887. There are several earlier references to the disease, notably one by Parry, of Bath, in 1825, but Hirschsprung's careful study established its existence as a definite clinical entity.

The Queen Louise Hospital for Children, Copenhagen. Circa 1900

Caleb Hillier Parry, 1755–1822. M.D. Edin., F.R.S. Physician, the General Hospital, Bath. In addition to describing Hirschsprung's disease before Hirschsprung, Parry described Graves' disease before Graves.

Harald Hirschsprung was born in Copenhagen, and qualified M.D. Copenhagen in 1855. In 1879 he was appointed head physician to the Queen Louise Children's Hospital in Copenhagen, and he became professor of diseases of children in 1877. Hirschsprung published many articles on subjects relating to children's diseases, especially on occlusion of the oesophagus and the small intestine, intussusception, rickets, and rheumatism.

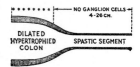

Hirschsprung's Disease

On the occasion of Harald Hirschsprung's seventieth birthday, in 1900, there was a great celebration in his honour and a marble bust was unveiled in the hospital that he had served for so many years.

In 1904 he retired from practice, and he died at home when in his seventy-seventh year.

Hirschsprung's paper on 'Constipation in the Newborn due to Dilatation and Hypertrophy of the Colon' was published in the *German Yearbook of Paediatrics* in 1887. He presented post-mortem specimens from two cases, together with the clinical histories, and speculated as to the cause of the condition.

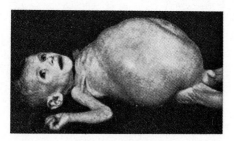

Hirschsprung's Disease

Sir Frederick Treves, 1853–1923. Surgeon, The London Hospital. In 1902 he operated successfully upon King Edward VII for an appendix abscess.
Orvass Swenson. Contemporary. Formerly Surgeon in Chief, Children's Memorial Hospital, Chicago, Illinois, U.S.A.

In 1898 Sir Frederick Treves attributed the cause of Hirschsprung's disease to congenital spasm of the distal segment, thus preceding Orvass Swenson's re-discovery of this concept by 50 years.

Particularly by the studies of Martin Bodian, the cause of the immotility of the spastic segment has become evident. There is an absence of parasympathetic ganglion cells, and this ganglion deficiency extends for a short distance into a transitional zone between the terminal spastic segment and the dilated and hypertrophied portions.

Martin Bodian, 1910–1963. Morbid Anatomist, Hospital for Sick Children, Great Ormond Street, London.

HODGKIN'S DISEASE

THOMAS HODGKIN
1798–1866

Thomas Hodgkin, the discoverer of Hodgkin's disease, was not appreciated in his day and generation. Indeed, he may be described as a failure. He failed to obtain a position on the staff of Guy's Hospital, and met with little success in private practice. He eventually gave up the practice of medicine altogether.

Thomas Hodgkin was born at Pentonville, London, the son of John Hodgkin, who was a fashionable tutor and instructed young ladies in mathematics, classics and especially handwriting, in which he excelled. John Hodgkin was a Quaker, and throughout life his son retained the distinctive dress and demeanour then characteristic of members of that sect. He studied medicine at Guy's Hospital and graduated M.D. Edinburgh in 1823. He then visited Paris and learned the use of the stethoscope from its inventor, that great physician, Laennec. Hodgkin was one of the first physicians in England to adopt what his contemporaries called 'a new-fangled contrivance.'

Hodgkin eschewed worldly matters. The tale is told that he sat up all night with a very wealthy man, who was ill and recovered. The patient was so grateful that he handed Hodgkin a blank cheque, telling him to fill it in for any amount he liked. Hodgkin entered ten pounds. The patient asked him why he put such a moderate amount. Hodgkin replied that he thought the drawer of the cheque looked as though he could not afford more. As a result the patient was so angry that he never again asked Hodgkin for his services.

Believing a study of pathology would help to make him a better physician Hodgkin became Curator of the Museum at Guy's Hospital, and in 1832 he read a paper with the title *On Some*

René-Théophile-Hyacinthe Laennec, 1781–1826. Physician, Hôpital Necker, Paris.

Morbid Appearances of the Absorbent Glands and Spleen, based on specimens of morbid anatomy that he had collected. The dissertation contained a description of that peculiar disease of lymph-nodes associated with enlargement of the spleen now known as Hodgkin's disease. In spite of the fact that the majority of these specimens were true examples of the disease that bears his name (as can be verified in the collection still preserved in Guy's Hospital)

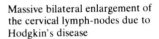

Massive bilateral enlargement of the cervical lymph-nodes due to Hodgkin's disease

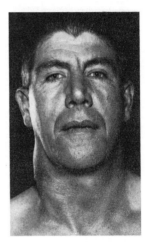

this article attracted little or no attention at the time. Thirty-three years later Sir Samuel Wilks disinterred it and added a considerable number of his own cases. It is greatly to Sir Samuel Wilks' credit that he called the condition Hodgkin's disease (1865).

Dejected by his repeated failure to obtain a position on the medical staff of Guy's Hospital, Hodgkin decided to abandon the practice of medicine, and thenceforth to devote himself to questions of reform and charitable works. He died of dysentery contracted at Jaffa, whither he had repaired on a mission of relief to the Jews. Thomas Hodgkin was buried in a small Protestant cemetery in Jaffa. His Jewish friend, Sir Moses Montefiore, arranged for an obelisk to be erected over the grave on which was inscribed: 'Here rests the body of Thomas Hodgkin, M.D. a man distinguished alike for scientific attainments, medical skills and self sacrificing philanthropy. He died at Jaffa the 4th April 1866, in the 68th year of his

Sir Samuel Wilks, 1824–1911. Physician, Guy's Hospital, London.

age, in the faith and hope of the Gospel.' Regretfully, today his grave is neglected and overgrown.

Doubtless, if the Governors of Guy's Hospital had appointed Hodgkin to their staff, medicine would have been enriched still further, for no young physician ever gave greater promise.

HORSLEY'S WAX

SIR VICTOR
HORSLEY
1857–1916

Horsley's Wax was the invention of Sir Victor Horsley, one of the founders of modern brain surgery. When Horsley commenced to specialise, cranial surgery had hardly advanced since the days of Ambroise Paré, in the sixteenth century. The only operation practised was trephining, which had been known since the Stone Age. Any further advance was impossible without a knowledge of brain physiology. In 1884 young Victor Horsley was appointed Professor-Superintendent to the Brown Institution of the University of London. This research building had been founded with money left in the will of a Mr. Thomas Brown of Dublin. The institution itself was destroyed in an air raid in 1944. Horsley performed extensive animal experiments on localisation of brain function in the monkey. He was the first to carry out experiments on the pituitary gland, showing that animals could survive its removal and linger on in a state of weakness. In addition to this extensive neurological experiments, he also demonstrated that removal of the thyroid gland in monkeys produced myxoedema and he also carried out studies on rabies.

In spite, however, of this advance in knowledge, many technical difficulties still remained to be surmounted before operations upon the brain could be undertaken with any degree of safety.

One of the difficulties to be surmounted was the haemorrhage from the cranial bones, which was extremely hard to control. Here again Horsley provided the answer by further animal experiments. He discovered that ordinary modelling wax smeared

Ambroise Paré, 1510–1590. After being apprenticed to a provincial barber-surgeon, and working as a dresser at the Hôtel Dieu, he became one of the greatest military surgeons of all time.

upon the raw edges of the cut skull bones would effectively control haemorrhage. With the help of P. W. Squire he evolved a wax which was antiseptic and answered the same purpose as the modelling preparation. The composition of this substance was: beeswax 7 parts, almond oil 1 part. Thus Horsley's wax came into being, and is still used in cranial surgery.

In 1914 Horsley made another momentous discovery. He found that troublesome haemorrhagic oozing from soft tissues, such as brain or liver, could be controlled by applying living muscle tissue to the bleeding surface and holding it there.

Victor Horsley was born in Kensington, London, the son of John Callcot Horsley, an artist of such merit as to receive the distinction of R.A. He was an opponent of the pre-Raphaelites, and he won especial favour among the prudish mid-Victorians by strongly opposing the employment of nude artist's models. Victor was

University College Hospital in 1880. It was then called the
North London Hospital

brought up at his father's country house near Cranbrook, Kent, where he attended the Elizabethan school at Cranbrook as a day boy. On leaving school he entered University College, London, as a medical student. After a brilliant undergraduate career he qualified M.B., B.S. (Lond.), taking the Gold Medal in Surgery in 1881. His brilliance was such that after serving the hospital in several junior appointments he was elected surgeon to University College Hospital and also to the National Hospital, Queen Square. In 1887 he successfully removed a tumour of the spinal cord with complete recovery of his paraplegic patient. This was the first operation of its

Sir Peter Wyatt Squire, 1846–1919. Pharmacist. The son of Peter Squire of Squire's Companion to the Pharmacopoea, *the later editions of which Sir Peter edited. He was knighted because he had acted for many years as pharmacist to the Royal Household.*

kind ever to be performed, and was a landmark in the history of surgery.

Apart from his professional activities, he was keenly interested in sociology and politics, and strongly supported women's suffrage. He was a fierce opponent of the use of tobacco and alcohol. It was his belief that it was the ingestion of alcohol rather than the sun *per se* that caused heat-stroke, and to prove his theory he went about without a sun-helmet in the tropical sun. He died of heat-stroke in 1916 while serving with the Royal Army Medical Corps in Mesopotamia, and was buried with military honours at Amara.

HUTCHINSON'S TEETH

HUTCHINSON'S PUPILS

SIR
JONATHAN
HUTCHINSON
1828–1913

Jonathan Hutchinson was born at Selby, Yorkshire, the son of a prosperous middleman in the flax trade. The family being Quakers, in accordance with the practice of the Society of Friends, Jonathan was educated at home until the age of 17, when he was apprenticed to a doctor of York. At the age of 21 he came to London, and entered St. Bartholomew's Hospital to work under James Paget. While acting as a dresser in the Out-patient Department Hutchinson noticed two juvenile patients suffering from an identical chronic inflammation of the eyes. Both these children had stigmata of syphilis, but at that time interstitial keratitis (as Jonathan Hutchinson subsequently named it) was not considered to be of syphilitic origin.

Jonathan Hutchinson qualified M.R.C.S. (Eng.) in 1850. Thus qualified he obtained the post of house-surgeon at the County Hospital, York. Six months later he returned to London, determined to gain a special knowledge of diseases of the eye, and to this end he attended several hospitals with ophthalmic departments. During this time he was dependent on an allowance from home, and in order to save his father expense, he sustained himself on a diet of bread and figs. While undertaking this postgraduate study, he contributed weekly to the *Medical Times* a column entitled *Reports from the Hospitals* for which, no doubt, he received a small remuneration. At the age of 25 Hutchinson succeeded in being appointed surgeon to both the Hospital for Diseases of the Skin,

Sir James Paget (see p. 179).

Blackfriars, and to the Metropolitan Hospital. At this point he changed his way of life. Having married, he went to live at Reigate, Surrey, and had consulting rooms in Finsbury Circus, in the heart of the City of London. In 1858 he published his epoch-making paper on interstitial keratitis, and to the original two he had observed as a dresser he had added no less than 62 more cases. Later in life he elaborated this thesis still further to embrace other stigmata of congenital syphilis. These included the pegtop incisor teeth (now known the world over as Hutchinson's teeth) and deafness. He also framed his triad of signs of congenital syphilis, to wit, 8th nerve deafness, Hutchinson's teeth and interstitial keratitis.

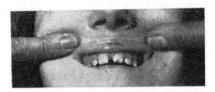

Hutchinson's teeth. The left central
incisor is characteristic

In 1860 he was appointed assistant surgeon to the London Hospital, and he moved from Reigate to reside in Finsbury Circus. In 1862 he was elected F.R.C.S. (Eng.), and in the following year was appointed surgeon to Moorfields Eye Hospital.

In January, 1865, Jonathan Hutchinson won the Astley Cooper prize of £300 for an essay *On Injuries of the Head and Their Treatment*, in which he described the original observation that in extradural haemorrhage, as the compression of the brain increases, the pupil of the same side undergoes increasing dilatation, and becomes increasingly inactive to a bright light. This phenomenon is due to compression of the IIIrd cranial (oculomotor) nerve against the tentorium cerebelli. This nerve transmits the parasympathetic constrictor fibres to the pupil; as these are paralysed, the unopposed sympathetic fibres dilate the pupil. This proved, and has continued to prove, of signal service in the diagnosis of traumatic extradural haemorrhage.

Another condition that remains associated with his name is the 'Potato tumour' of Jonathan Hutchinson (carotid body tumour).

Sir Astley Cooper, 1768-1841. Surgeon, Guy's Hospital, London.

The potato-tumour of Jonathan Hutchinson

Jonathan Hutchinson, by his tremendous industry, unrivalled powers of observation, lucid writings and thronged lectures to students and medical societies, became one of the leading figures in the profession of his day. Mainly an ophthalmologist, a dermatologist and a syphilologist, his interests extended beyond these

Hutchinson's pupil. Side of lesion dilated

spheres, any one of which might have been a life's work for a more ordinary man. In spite of being one of London's best-known consultants, Jonathan Hutchinson did not move from the City of London to the West End until his forty-seventh year, and he did so then only on the advice of his former teacher, Sir James Paget.

In his prime Hutchinson was described as being above middle height, possessing dark eyes that seemed to look past one over his spectacles, black hair, and a black beard. He was an insatiable collector, and formed a vast museum of specimens, coloured drawings, and charts. He wrote numerous books, and published 10 volumes of *Archives of Surgery* in periodical form; the entire contents of these volumes were written by himself.

In 1882 he was elected a Fellow of the Royal Society, and in 1889 President of the Royal College of Surgeons. He was knighted in 1908.

JACKSONIAN
EPILEPSY

JOHN
HUGHLINGS
JACKSON
1835–1911

By Jacksonian epilepsy is understood the occurrence of fits commencing in one group of muscles. Usually the spasms are limited to one side of the body. Sometimes this form of epilepsy is a consequence of an injury to the brain, viz. blood clot, a depressed fracture or a spicule of bone pressing upon the motor cortex of one side of the brain, with the result that seizures occur on the opposite side of the body. If, for instance, that part of the cerebral cortex which controls the forearm is the part that is irritated, the fit will start in the forearm—an important diagnostic feature. Jacksonian epilepsy can also result from a tumour of the brain involving the motor cortex. Cortical epilepsy, with its peculiarities of focal attacks, clonic spasms and *late* loss of consciousness—a discovery that brought Hughlings Jackson immortal fame—was described in 1875.

John Hughlings Jackson was born in the Yorkshire village of Green Hammerton, the son of a farmer who was also a small brewer. After attending nearby schools, John was apprenticed to a practitioner in York where at that time there was a small medical school, which had but a short existence. From York Medical School Hughlings Jackson proceded to St. Bartholomew's Hospital, London, and he qualified M.R.C.S. and L.S.A. in 1856. Returning to York as house-surgeon, he remained in that city until 1859. He then decided to migrate to London, and armed with an introduction to Jonathan Hutchinson, who also came from York, he made rapid progress in the capital city. In a matter of months Hughlings

Sir Jonathan Hutchinson (see p. 110).

Jackson was appointed Lecturer in Pathology at the London Hospital, and having taken the M.D. St. Andrews and the M.R.C.P. London, he was elected assistant physician to the London Hospital. It is said that Jackson's determination to specialise in neurology came about when he himself suffered an attack of Bell's palsy. Be that as it may, he was appointed assistant physician to the National Hospital for Nervous Diseases, Queen Square, in 1862.

The National Hospital, Queen Square, London

Hughlings Jackson did much to establish the use of the ophthalmoscope in the diagnosis of brain disease. He made notable advances in the understanding of aphasia. In 1875 he originated the doctrine of levels in the central nervous system. Unfortunately his style of writing was far from clear. Students turned away from the bristling difficulties of reading Hughling Jackson's numerous papers. As a consequence many of his most notable observations remained unappreciated until years later when his brilliant pupils expounded them.

When he was 30 years of age Hughlings Jackson married his cousin, and 11 years later, by the irony of fate, she died of cerebral thrombosis associated with Jacksonian epilepsy. After her death he became more shy, and rather eccentric. When he read a book he would tear out those pages that interested him, and throw the remainder away. On one occasion be bought a book at a railway station, tore it in half, ripped off the covers, and handed them to

Sir Charles Bell (see p. 10).

the astonished assistant. Placing one half of the coverless book in each pocket of his overcoat, he proceeded to catch the train.

Hughlings Jackson died of pneumonia at the age of 76 years. His many advancements of neurology receive greater recognition today than they did in his lifetime.

KLUMPKE'S PARALYSIS

MADAME
DÉJERINE-
KLUMPKE
1859–1927

In 1877 four sisters, the Misses Klumpke, arrived in Paris from Lausanne. They were of American origin, having been born in San Francisco, but had been educated in Switzerland.

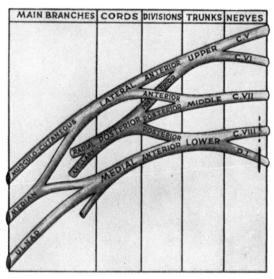

Showing the lesion in Klumpke's Paralysis.
C.viii is sometimes involved

Auguste Klumpke, the future physician, was the most famous of the four, though all the sisters displayed great ability and became well known in Paris, one as an artist, another as a musician, and the third as a Doctor of Science.

Auguste decided to enter the medical profession. Those were pioneer days for medical women, and she had a hard struggle to overcome the prejudices of the French teachers. Eventually her importunity was rewarded, and the Professor of Medicine accepted her as a student in the Medical Faculty of the University of Paris.

The principal entrance to the University of Paris. On the right is the medical wing

Miss Klumpke proved a model pupil. Her brilliance was extraordinary. While a student, she described what is known today as Klumpke's Paralysis.

This, as she described, is a lesion of the lower trunk or the medial cord of the brachial plexus caused by such accidents as clutching at a ledge by a falling person, failing to obtain a foothold on a passing bus, or by an unreduced dislocation of the humerus. The injury leads to wasting of all the small muscles of the hand (claw hand), together with a sensory impairment of the inner 3½ fingers and the ulnar side of the forearm. She also recorded that the lesion may be associated with Horner's syndrome, with constriction of the pupil and ptosis, due to injury of the adjacent stellate ganglion.

In the course of her studies Miss Klumpke made the acquaintance of Jules Déjerine, a rising young neurologist. She married him while she was a final-year student. She obtained her M.D. degree in 1888. Known as Madame Déjerine-Klumpke, she helped her

Johann Friedrich Horner, 1831–1886. Professor of Ophthalmology, Zurich. Described the syndrome in 1869.
Jules Déjerine, 1849–1917. Clinical Chief at the Salpêtrière, Paris.

husband in his great work on the anatomy of the central nervous system, and when he died in 1917 she founded a laboratory to perpetuate his memory and to carry on his research work. Held in esteem throughout France, she was President of the Société de Neurologie and an Officer of the Legion of Honour. She died in 1927 at the age of 68 years, leaving one daughter, who married a French surgeon.

KOCH'S
BACILLUS

KOCH'S
POSTULATES

ROBERT
KOCH
1843–1910

The life of Robert Koch is perhaps the most inspiring of any in this book. Robert Koch was the son of a mining engineer, and was born at Klausthal, in Hanover, on 11th December, 1843. After receiving his education at the local gymnasium, he studied at Göttingen and took the M.D. in 1866. Soon afterwards he went into general practice at Langenhagen, near Hanover. In 1870 he served as a surgeon in the Franco-Prussian war and, on leaving the army at the close of the war, he obtained the Diploma of Public Health, and combined the duties of Medical Officer of Health with those of general practice at Wollstein, in Posen.

The career of Robert Koch is a classic example of what can be achieved by application and perseverance. Far away from the stimulus of a university and laboratories, he devoted himself to microscopical study.

In 1876, while in the midst of his country practice, Koch published an epoch-making paper on the anthrax bacillus. He

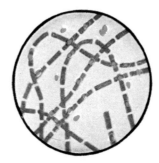

Anthrax bacilli showing spores. Koch's first great essay in bacteriology

119

showed that the anthrax bacilli grew in long chains, and that the bacilli formed spores which retained their virulence for years.

Hardly can it be appreciated today that this was the very first paper in the world to allege that an infectious disease can be, and often is, caused by a definite micro-organism: Koch proved that it could be beyond all possibility of doubt. As a country doctor, Koch had formulated a hypothesis that was confirmed by the great Pasteur, and Pasteur himself hailed the discovery as the greatest yet made in bacteriology. Every reader, and especially every isolated practitioner, will do well to dwell for a moment on this inspiring thought. The following year, Koch published his method of fixing and staining bacteria. Other papers, which elevated him to the front rank in medical science, quickly followed. He was appointed to the staff of the Imperial Health Department so that he could continue his researches.

In 1881 Koch demonstrated the first pure cultures of bacteria at the International Medical Congress in London. After the lecture the great Pasteur rushed forward with the exclamation: *'C'est un grand progrès!'*

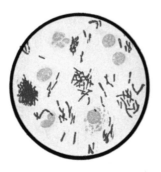

Mycobacterium tuberculosis also known as Koch's bacilli. The discovery of the cause of tuberculosis was the crowning glory of Koch's life

It was on 24th March, 1882, that Koch announced to the Berlin Physiological Society his discovery of the *Mycobacterium tuberculosis*.

Koch defined the three conditions which need to be fulfilled in order to justify the conclusion that a particular disease is called by a particular organism. These three 'Koch's Postulates' are:

1. The organism should be found in all cases of the disease and

Louis Pasteur, 1822–1895. World-famous French chemist and bacteriologist. (He was a D.Sc., but was not qualified medically.) Founder of the Pasteur Institute, Paris.

its distribution in the body should accord with the observed lesions.

2. The organism should be cultivated outside the host and sub-cultured for several generations.

3. The organism isolated in these sub-cultures should then reproduce the disease when transmitted to other hosts.

In 1885 he was offered and accepted the appointment of Professor of Hygiene at the University of Berlin. Wedded as he was to research, it did not suit him to spend his days teaching students and after a few years he resigned from the professorship. A post was created for him—that of chief of the Institute for Infectious Diseases—where he could follow his inclinations.

The Robert Koch Institute, Berlin, completed in 1901.
Within its walls are preserved the ashes of Robert Koch

Koch returned again and again to the problem of tuberculosis. World-wide excitement was caused when in 1890 he announced his discovery of Tuberculin, although hopes that inoculation of this extract of the bacillus might cure tuberculosis were not later confirmed. Koch travelled all over the world studying epidemics. At the request of the British Government he went to India* and carried out important work on bubonic plague. He proved that the malady was transmitted to human beings by the rat-flea. He studied

* This was his second visit to India; on the first visit in 1883 he discovered the cause of cholera, the *Vibrio cholerae*. When he returned home he was awarded a National prize of 100,000 marks.

the tsetse-fly in German East Africa, and went to Ceylon for researches in malaria. In 1906 he visited South Africa as head of the Sleeping Sickness Commission.

In 1905 the Nobel Prize for medicine was awarded to him.

In appearance Koch was a typical Prussian savant, a man of unceasing industry, dignified and modest. Undoubtedly he was one of the greatest men of science his country has ever produced. He died of heart failure at the age of 67. By his own wish his body was cremated and the ashes deposited in his Institute at Berlin.

The importance of Koch's discoveries cannot be exaggerated, and there are few to whom medicine owes so much.

KOCHER'S INCISIONS
for thyroidectomy and
cholecystectomy
MANOEUVRE
for dislocated shoulder
MANOEUVRE
for mobilisation of the
duodenum
ARTERY CLAMP
GLAND DISSECTOR
THYROID RETRACTOR

THEODOR
KOCHER
1841–1917

Theodor Kocher was Switzerland's greatest surgeon, whose important contributions ranged widely over the whole field of surgery. He
is a member of the élite club of surgeons who have received the
Nobel Prize.

Kocher was born in Bern, the son of a distinguished engineer,
and it was in Bern that he spent nearly the whole of his professional
life. After graduation from the University of that city, he visited
clinics in Berlin, Vienna, Paris and London, including those of
Billroth, Lister and Spencer Wells. Returning to the surgical clinic
of his University, Kocher was promoted to Professor at the early
age of 31 and remained in that position for the next 45 years, dying
in harness at the age of 76.

His textbook *Operative Surgery* was immensely popular and was
translated into several languages. His profound knowledge of
anatomy is demonstrated by its details of surgical approaches to all
the major joints. In it he also described his well-known subcostal
incision for exposure of the gall-bladder which is still frequently
used to this day. He popularised the collar incision for thyroidectomy which bears his name and which replaced the ugly vertical
midline incision used by previous surgeons. In it he also describes
the technique for mobilisation of the duodenum by division of its

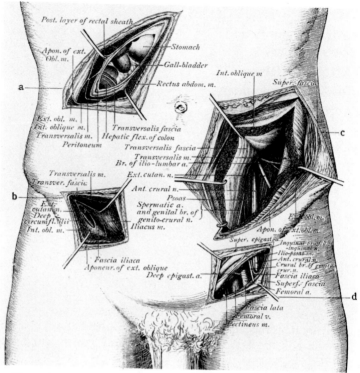

Illustration from Kocher's *Operative Surgery* of various abdominal incisions including the subcostal exposure of the gall bladder

lateral peritoneal attachments, for which American surgeons have invented the phrase 'Kocherisation of the duodenum.'

In 1870 he wrote a long article describing his method of reduction of a dislocated shoulder, still popular today, which could be carried out almost painlessly, without anaesthesia or assistance:

'Bend the arm at the elbow, press it against the body, rotate outwards till a resistance is felt, lift the externally rotated upper arm in the sagittal plane as far as possible forwards, and finally turn inwards slowly.'

However, it was Kocher's contributions to the surgery of the thyroid gland which constitute his greatest claim to fame and earned him his Nobel Prize in 1909. Switzerland, being mountainous and land-bound, is an iodine-deficient region; enormous goitres, often associated with cretinism, were endemic before iodination of table salt was introduced. There was, therefore, a tremendous pool of patients requiring Kocher's meticulous surgical technique which he developed for thyroidectomy. His mortality rate fell from 12·8 per cent in 1883 to less than 0·5 per cent and, in one consecutive series of 600 cases, there was but a single death.

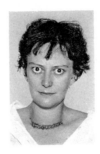

The collar incision for thyroidectomy

At the start of his surgical career very little was known of the function of the thyroid and, in his early series, Kocher performed total thyroidectomies in the majority of cases. However, Reverdin of Geneva reported that patients subjected to total thyroidectomy developed a condition which was soon identified as being similar to cretinism and myxoedema. Kocher reviewed his own patients and confirmed this finding on those submitted to total thyroidectomy. Patients who had only had partial resections escaped this condition, which Kocher named 'cachexia strumipriva.' He wrote:

'As a rule, soon after discharge from the hospital, but in occasional cases not before the lapse of four or five months, the patients begin to complain of fatigue, and especially of weakness and heaviness in the extremities . . . In addition there is a sensation of coldness. The mental alertness decreases. Children who were formerly among the brightest pupils suddenly fall back. There is gradually increasing slowness of speech and of all other movements . . . If we are to give a name to this picture we cannot fail to recognise its relation to idiocy and cretinism; the stunted growth, the large head, the swollen nose, thick lips, heavy body and clumsiness of thought and speech undoubtedly point to a related evil.'

The importance of the thyroid gland to normal life was estab-

Jacques Louis Reverdin, 1842–1929. Professor of Surgery, Geneva. First pointed out the close resemblance between patients following total thyroidectomy and cases of myxoedema.

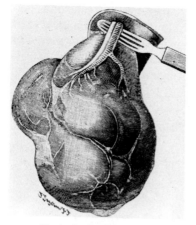

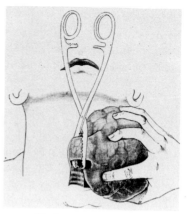

Kocher's gland dissector   Kocher's pedicle forceps
(illustration from his *Operative Surgery*)

lished and from then on Kocher carried out only sub-total resections for benign thyroid disease.

It was Felix Semon, a laryngologist at St. Thomas' Hospital, who concluded in 1883 that cachexia strumipriva, myxoedema and cretinism were all due to the same cause, loss of thyroid function, and this was confirmed by the animal studies of Victor Horsley at the Brown Institution (see p. 107).

Many of the instruments we use today in thyroid surgery were invented by Kocher—his gland dissector, his pedicle artery forceps, provided with a 'rat-tooth' at their tips, and his self-retaining thyroid retractor.

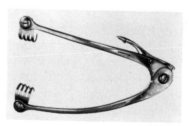

Kocher's self-retaining thyroid retractors

Sir Felix Semon, 1849–1921. Laryngologist, St. Thomas' Hospital, London.
Sir Victor Horsley (see p. 107).

Kocher was a master surgeon who preached careful diagnosis and gentle precise operative technique. He was a serene person and the atmosphere of serenity pervaded his operating theatre. Truly he was one of Switzerland's finest sons.

KOPLIK'S SPOTS

HENRY KOPLIK 1858–1927

'It is indeed very late in the day to describe something new connected with the exanthemata,' said Henry Koplik in the original description of Koplik's spots which is to be found in an article in the *Archives of Pediatrics* of New York, 1896, *13*, 918, having made his observations at the Good Samaritan Dispensary, New York. At the time Koplik was 38 years old.

After describing the prodromal symptoms of measles, Dr. Koplik continues: 'On the buccal mucous membrane and the inside of the lips we invariably see a distinct eruption. It consists of small,

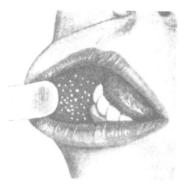

Koplik's Spots

irregular spots, of a bright red colour. In the centre of each spot there is noted, in strong daylight, a minute bluish-white speck. These red spots, with accompanying specks of a bluish-white colour, are absolutely pathognomonic of beginning measles, and when seen can be relied upon as the forerunner of the skin eruption.' Typically the spots appear on the second day of the fever, the rash not appearing till the fourth day. Presumably they occur throughout the gastro-intestinal tract because they have been observed on the exposed mucosa of a colostomy!

Two years later Dr. Koplik published a second paper on the same subject and recorded 16 cases which were diagnosed by the aid of 'my spots.'

Measles had been studied for centuries, but no physician before Koplik appears to have realised the importance of these spots as a diagnostic sign.

Even after the publication of Koplik's papers a considerable time elapsed before the sign became well known, and, as so often happens, it had a better reception abroad than in the country of its origin. It has been well said that the history of measles may be divided into *before* and *after* Koplik. At the present time Koplik's spots are recognised by every medical practitioner and every medical student the world over as being a pathognomic sign of measles, but how many know that the man whose Eastern European name they perpetuate was born, bred and worked in New York City?

Henry Koplik was born in New York City. He was educated at the College of the City of New York and at Columbia University, and after taking his medical degree in 1881, he studied in Berlin, Vienna and Prague. Almost the whole of his professional life was spent in the study of children's diseases. For 25 years he was Attending Paediatrician to the Mount Sinai Hospital, New York.

He was one of the founders and sometime President of the American Pediatric Society. In 1889, at the Good Samaritan Dispensary, he established the first sterilised milk depot for infants in America.

His book on *The Diseases of Infancy and Childhood* appeared in 1902 and went through four later editions.

A big, bluff, good-natured man, with a white Vandyke beard, he was one of the most popular as well as respected physicians of New York.

He died of a coronary thrombosis while in his sixty-ninth year.

LANE'S PLATES
LANE'S INTESTINAL CLAMPS
LANE'S TISSUE FORCEPS

SIR WILLIAM ARBUTHNOT LANE
1856–1943

Arbuthnot Lane was a brilliant technical surgeon whose dexterity was probably only equalled by Moynihan. He made many important contributions to surgery but he was not himself a great initiator of ideas, rather he adapted and popularised many important aspects of surgical technique. Undoubtedly his greatest contribution was his work on the open fixation of fractures. This was not a new concept, of course; Lister himself, for example, had carried out wiring of the fractured patella. However, it was Lane who pioneered the use of screw fixation of fractures, which he commenced in 1893,

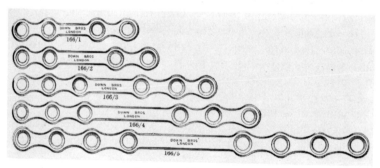

Lane's steel bone plates

Lord Moynihan (see p. 170).
Lord Lister (see p. 139).

and by 1905 he had introduced his special perforated steel strips (Lane's plates) for plating fractures of the long bones.

Of course, any infection in such instances would prove disastrous and, in other hands, there were many failures. Lane, however, introduced the strictest asepsis into his theatres, the 'no touch technique.' For this he devised long artery and dissecting forceps so that, even in the deepest wound, the fingers that held them could not touch the wound edges. The sutures were never touched but were threaded using two pairs of dissecting forceps. This asepsis was combined with meticulous haemostasis and the gentlest handling of the tissues.

Although in his day Lane came in for heavy criticism for converting closed fractures into open wounds, modern operative orthopaedic surgery owes a great deal to his early efforts.

Lane was born in 1846 at Fort St. George, Scotland. He was the son of an army surgeon and as a child he accompanied his parents to India, Corfu, Malta (where one of his brothers died of cholera) and Nova Scotia. He entered Guy's Hospital at the early age of 16 and spent long hours in the dissecting room, being appointed an Assistant Demonstrator while still a student. Willie, as he was known to all his family and friends throughout his life, qualified in 1877 at the age of 21 and was appointed House Surgeon to the Victoria Hospital for Children, Tite Street, in Chelsea and it was here that he made his first contribution to operative surgery: he published five cases of rib resection for chronic empyema in children with four successes. In 1882 he returned to Guy's as Demonstrator of Anatomy and stayed there until 1887 while serving at the same time on the staff of the Hospital for Sick Children, Great Ormond Street. Lane liked nothing better than to demonstrate his prowess as a dissector. Indeed the students would say, 'Don't let Lane touch your part or you will have nothing of it left.' His careful dissections, often carried out late into the night, demonstrated how the skeleton might undergo curvature in relation to prolonged heavy labour and he coined the term 'the skeleton represents crystallisation of lines of force.' He published papers on the anatomy of the charwoman and the shoemaker.

While still a Demonstrator on a salary of £200 a year he married and had a happy family life with three daughters and a son.

In 1888 he was elected to the staff at Guy's Hospital and served it until his retirement in 1920.

At Guy's and Great Ormond Street he made important technical advances in many branches of surgery. He introduced exploration of the mastoid antrum in the treatment of chronic purulent otitis media, for which he devised special chisels and gouges. He devised an ingenious flap operation for cleft palate repair and advocated operation in the earliest weeks of life, inventing special fine needles to suture the delicate tissues. He was the first to treat septic thrombosis of the lateral sinus complicating aural sepsis by ligature of the internal jugular vein and removal of the septic thrombus. This he carried out in August 1888, the child being a descendant of Admiral Nelson. He was an early advocate of the use of saline for transfusion in haemorrhage in the days before blood was available. In 1896 he reported the successful removal of a brain tumour and in 1909 he developed an operation for excision of cancer of the cervical oesophagus with repair of the defect by means of skin flaps.

Among Lane's achievements must be placed the fact that he was the first to perform a successful cardiac massage, which he reported

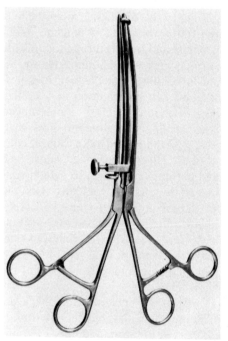

Lane's twin intestinal clamps for bowel anastomosis

in 1902. The patient was a man of 65, undergoing appendicectomy:

'During the trimming of the stump both pulse and respirations stopped together. Artificial respiration and traction on the tongue were performed without result. Then the surgeon introduced his hand through the abdominal incision and felt the motionless heart through the diaphragm. He gave it a squeeze or two and felt it restart beating.'

The operation was completed and the patient recovered fully. Lane also devised the simpler method of resuscitation in small infants by squeezing directly on the elastic chest wall.

Lane was deeply interested in abdominal surgery. He devised his non-crushing intestinal twin clamps which could be screwed together enabling side to side anastomoses between loops of bowel to be made with ease and this instrument is still in daily use in our operating theatres, as are his tissue forceps.

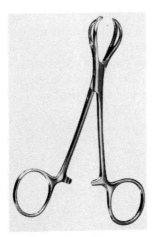

Lane's tissue forceps

Early in the 20th Century, Lane started to become obsessed with the idea of chronic constipation producing toxaemia and being the cause of many of the ills of civilisation. He believed, 'We suffer and die through the defects that arise in our sewerage and drainage system.' He first carried out short-circuiting of the large intestine in such cases (which came to be known as 'Lane's operation'), and then went even further and carried out total colectomies in patients suffering from such conditions as migraine and rheumatism. Fortunately, at a later date Lane preached that one might keep the colon as long as it was kept empty and introduced liquid paraffin, which at least was safer to the patient than having a total colectomy! Naturally, his views met with considerable opposition. Eventually, Lane took his name off the Medical Register in order to be able to address the public by lectures and through the press on his ideas for health. He was indeed a pioneer in what we now call Social Medicine. He founded the New Health Society, whose principal aims were to teach the public the simple laws of health, to attempt to make fruit and vegetables abundant and cheap for the general public and to encourage people to go back to the land. He started the journal *New Health* in 1926 and wrote a popular book *New Health for Every Man* when he was 75 years of age.

Lane was created a Baronet in 1913. During the First World War he became a consultant surgeon in the army and organised the Queen's Hospital at Sidcup for the treatment of facial injuries. It was here with a young New Zealander, Harold Gillies, that the foundations of modern plastic reconstructive surgery were laid.

Willie's first wife died in 1935, six months after their Golden Wedding. In the same year, he re-married, at the age of 79, and went on lecturing until the outbreak of World War II. Even then he went daily to the Athenaeum to read the papers. He died on 16th January, 1943 at the age of 86.

Sir Harold Delf Gillies, 1882–1960. New Zealand-born pioneer of plastic surgery in both World Wars. Consultant Surgeon, St. Bartholomew's Hospital, London.

LEISHMAN-DONOVAN BODIES

SIR WILLIAM
BOOG
LEISHMAN
1865–1926

CHARLES
DONOVAN
1863–1951

General Sir William Leishman

Leishman-Donovan bodies are small round or oval bodies found in the spleen, bone marrow and liver of patients suffering from kala-azar, a tropical disease characterised by anaemia, irregularly remittent fever and emaciation. The bodies are the intracellular forms of the protozoan parasite *Leishmania donovani*, which causes the disease.

Leishman-Donovan bodies in a
smear of bone marrow (×720)

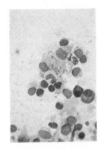

William Boog Leishman was born in Glasgow, the son of William Leishman, a distinguished obstetrician of that city. William Leishman, junior, was educated at Westminster School and at the University of Glasgow, where he graduated M.B., C.M. in 1886. In 1887 he entered the army medical service, and he spent several years in India before being posted, in 1899, to the Army Medical

William Leishman, 1833–1894. Regius Professor of Midwifery, Glasgow.

135

School at Netley. He had taken with him to India a microscope and had grasped every opportunity of becoming proficient in its use. At Netley he spent a great deal of his spare time in the pathological department, then under the direction of (Sir) Almroth Wright. He was able to watch the development of Wright's researches on anti-typhoid vaccination, in which he was later to take an important part. In 1900 he was appointed Assistant Professor of Pathology at Netley, and at this time he elaborated the stain for blood, now known universally as Leishman's stain.

Leishman made his great discovery in the following way:

> In 1900, Private B., invalided from India with attacks of pyrexia, anaemia and enlargement of the spleen, was admitted to Netley Hospital for investigation and treatment. Among other examinations, Leishman performed splenic puncture, stained the resulting specimen with his stain, and saw an enormous number of heavily stained round and oval bodies in the splenic cells and in the red blood cells. He searched the literature, but could find no comparable finding, and he was nonplussed. Many months later he was examining the blood, liver and spleen of a rat dead of trypanosomiasis; bodies identical in shape, size and staining reaction to those found in the case of Private B. were unmistakably present.

It was now 1903, and he published a short note of his findings in the *British Medical Journal*. Captain Charles Donovan confirmed the findings in Madras. Sir Ronald Ross the same year proposed that the bodies be called *Leishman-Donovan bodies*, and the parasite *Leishmania donovani*, and this nomenclature has been adopted throughout the world.

Thereafter Leishman made a number of other important discoveries in the field of tropical medicine. He rose rapidly to the highest ranks that the Royal Army Medical Corps can offer, and after filling with distinction the Chair of Pathology at Millbank Military Hospital, he became Director General of the Army Medical Services. He received the honour of Knighthood in 1909 and was elected a Fellow of the Royal Society in 1910. In 1926 General Sir William Leishman died at the age of 61 years, after a short illness.

Charles Donovan graduated M.D. at the Royal University of Ireland in 1889. Soon after qualification he entered the Indian Medical Service. At the time that he confirmed Leishman's discovery (1903) he was a Captain, and was second physician at the

Sir Almroth Wright, 1861–1947. Professor of Bacteriology, St. Mary's Hospital, London. Pioneer of anti-typhoid inoculation.

Sir Ronald Ross, 1857–1932. Director, Ross Institute for Tropical Diseases, London, proved that malaria was carried by the anopheles mosquito.

Lieutenant-Colonel Charles Donovan

Government General Hospital, Madras. It must not be lost sight of that in 1905 Charles Donovan made a discovery of even greater moment that that with which his name is jointly associated, and which has been described above. Donovan quite independently found the cause of granuloma inguinale (syn. granuloma venereum), a venereal disease rarely seen in England until the West Indians began to immigrate in substantial numbers (1956–1958). Granuloma inguinale, which must not be confused with lymphogranuloma inguinale, is caused by the *Donovania granulomatis*, a Donovan body found characteristically in the cytoplasm of white blood cells, particularly the large mononuclear leucocytes. Granuloma inguin-

Granuloma inguinale

ale gives rise to a painless swelling, or bubo, which later breaks down to form an ulcer, predominantly in the inguinal region.

In 1906 Major Donovan was appointed Civil Superintendent of Royapettah Hospital—a post that carried with it responsibility for the medical care of Government servants living in the district of Madras city. This hospital had 80 beds, and the post suited Donovan's independent character and gave him leisure to pursue research. In addition he held the post of Professor of Physiology at Madras College.

Apart from the great discoveries described above, Donovan was convinced that carriers of many of the tropical diseases in the Madras Residency were to be found among the denizens of the jungle, and he spent his holidays collecting blood slides to prove the existence of monkey malaria.

It is truly remarkable that while his co-discoverer in the Army was promoted with unprecedented rapidity, Donovan in the I.M.S. remained a Lieutenant-Colonel. Possibly it was for this reason that in 1920, when he was 57 years old, he resigned, and went to live in the village of Bourton-on-the-Water, Gloucestershire, where he died at the age of 88 years.

LISTER'S SINUS FORCEPS

LISTER'S TUBERCLE

LORD
LISTER
1827–1912

Lister was undoubtedly the greatest surgical benefactor of mankind. Indeed, we classify surgery into its pre- and post-Listerian eras. Before Lister, it was almost unknown for a surgical wound to heal primarily—suppuration was the norm. But local sepsis was the least of the dangers; septicaemia, pyaemia, erysipelas, tetanus and gas gangrene would sweep through the surgical wards. Hospital gangrene, a condition now no longer seen, was perhaps the most dreaded of all complications; the tissues around the wound would become grey or black, the process would spread rapidly and death was almost inevitable. Surgeons expected to lose a third of their cases of amputation and one is not surprised that usually operations were only resorted to as a last resort. It was Lister's work that changed all this and heralded the modern age of surgery. It is perhaps surprising that his name is only perpetuated eponymously in a useful dressing instrument which he devised and the dorsal tubercle on the posterior surface of the distal end of the radius adjacent to the groove for extensor pollicis longus.

Joseph Lister was born in 1827 in the pleasant country property of Upton Park in the Parish of West Ham in Essex, today the site is a block of council flats called Joseph Lister Court in the East End of London. His father, Joseph Jackson Lister, was a prosperous Quaker wine merchant and a distinguished amateur microscopist. He developed the achromatic microscope which gained him the Fellowship of the Royal Society.

139

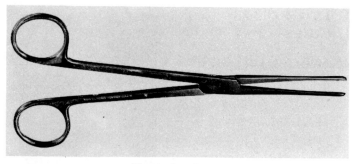

Lister's sinus forceps

In 1844, young Joseph, aged 16, entered University College, the 'Godless college,' which took members of any religious belief; unlike Oxford and Cambridge, where membership of the Church of England was obligatory. Here he took his B.A. in Arts but switched to Medicine and graduated M.B. in 1852; in the same year he achieved his F.R.C.S. He obviously inherited his father's interest in the microscope and in 1853 made the discovery that the involuntary muscle of the iris contained both dilator and constrictor fibres.

In September 1853, at the age of 26, Lister went on what was intended to be a short visit to study under James Syme, Professor of Clinical Surgery at the Edinburgh Royal Infirmary; in fact he was to stay in Scotland for many years. Syme and Lister were immediately attracted to each other; the young man was rapidly appointed his House Surgeon and within a year Lister was appointed to the surgical staff. At the same time, he married Agnes Syme, his chief's eldest daughter. Although they had no children, this was an ideal partnership of 37 years.

In 1860, Lister was appointed Professor of Surgery in the University of Glasgow and a year later took charge of beds at the Glasgow Royal Infirmary. It was at Glasgow that Lister entered his most productive period. He devised his screw tourniquet for compressing the abdominal aorta, a hook for removing foreign bodies from the ear, scissors with blunt probe-shaped tips for cutting bandages and his forceps for probing and packing narrow sinuses, which are in constant use to this day. In 1865 he published

James Syme (see p. 215).

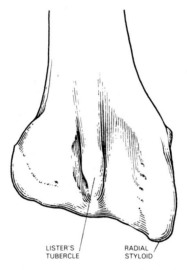

LISTER'S   RADIAL
TUBERCLE   STYLOID

The dorsal (Lister's) tubercle of the radius

his important paper on excision of the wrist for tuberculosis in the *Lancet*, a most valuable contribution, since it avoided amputation and left the patient with a tolerably useful hand. The dorsal tubercle on the distal extremity of the radius, a surgical landmark in this operation, now bears Lister's name.

Since his early days in Edinburgh, Lister had been interested in inflammation and it was there that he commenced his study on the microscopic changes accompanying inflammation which he carried out on the foot web of the frog. He was aware of Pasteur's work in 1864 which showed that broth would only putrefy when exposed to dusty city air but not to the clean air of the mountain top. Lister himself demonstrated that urine kept fresh when contained within a flask provided with an angled neck but decomposed in a straight-necked bottle which allowed contamination of the contents. Surely it was the 'germs,' as they were called, that produced putrefaction in wounds just as they produced fermentation in wine or decom-position of contaminated broth or urine. At this time no one had actually seen the bacteria which cause suppuration and it was to be some years before Robert Koch (see page 119) was to demonstrate that specific diseases could be attributed to specific organisms.

Louis Pasteur, 1825–1895. French Chemist and Bacteriologist.

The problem confronting Lister was to prevent germs from entering the wound. At this time there were newspaper accounts of the use of carbolic acid to purify the sewage in Carlisle and it was carbolic acid that Lister decided to use in his first clinical experiments. The crucial trial was on the 12th August 1865, when James Greenlees, aged 11, was admitted with a compound fracture of the left tibia. This was treated by a thorough cleaning with carbolic acid and then dressed with lint soaked in the solution. The result was a complete success and Lister wrote 'The remarkable retardation of suppuration and the immediate conversion of the compound fracture into a simple fracture with a superficial sore, were most encouraging.' Lister waited until 1867 to report his trial, by which time 11 patients had been treated for compound fractures with nine complete successes. One patient developed hospital gangrene during Lister's absence and required amputation and another, although progressing satisfactorily, died of haemorrhage as a result of perforation of the femoral artery by a fracture fragment. It can truly be said that the publication of these results marked the watershed between the old and the new era of surgery.

Lister's carbolic spray

Lister's statue in Portland Place, London

Lister went on to apply his technique to the drainage of tuberculous abscesses, the ligation of major vessels, for which he first used silk soaked in carbolic, and then switched to carbolic-treated catgut, and then, most daringly of all, open fixations of fractures of the patella and olecranon using silver wire.

It must be admitted that Lister's techniques were only slowly adopted by most British surgeons and were accepted more readily by his European colleagues. However, Lister devoted the rest of his clinical life to perfecting his techniques, experimenting with the use of a carbolic spray (much to the discomfort of the surgeon and his assistants) and the use of other antiseptics including perchloride of mercury and boric acid.

In 1869, his father-in-law Professor Syme had a stroke and Joseph Lister succeeded him as Professor of Surgery. In 1877 Lister was invited to become Professor of Surgery at King's College Hospital and decided to make the move to London in order to preach his antiseptic surgery in the Metropolis.

In his later years, Lister was showered with honours. He was created surgeon to Queen Victoria in 1878 and indeed drained her axillary abscess using the antiseptic principle—'a most unpleasant task, most pleasantly performed', the Queen said after the operation. In 1883 he was made a Baronet and in 1897 created a Peer, the first occasion in which a doctor had been so honoured. In 1895 he became President of the Royal Society (he had been made a Fellow at the early age of 33). He served on Council of the Royal College of Surgeons from 1880 to 1888 but was never its President.

Lister died peacefully on the 10th February 1912. He left clear instructions that he was to be buried beside Lady Lister in West Hampstead cemetery where there was a simple and private funeral. There is a fine statue in his memory in Portland Place, a short walk from his London home in Park Crescent, on which has been placed a commemorative plaque.

In the public memorial service in Westminster Abbey on February 16th 1912 the choir sang Handel's anthem, whose words were particularly appropriate:

'Kindness, meekness and comfort were in his tongue . . .

His body is buried in peace, but his name liveth evermore.'

LISTON'S BONE FORCEPS

LISTON'S SPLINT

ROBERT
LISTON
1794–1847

Liston's long splint is not now used in the treatment of fractures of the femur, but it was the standard treatment for such fractures for nearly a hundred years, the decline in its use commencing just prior to the 1914–18 war, during which period it was replaced by the Thomas splint. Liston's bone forceps are still in common use.

Robert Liston was born at Ecclesmachen in Linlithgowshire. Like many other great Scotsmen he was a son of the manse.

In 1810, at the age of 16, Liston went to Edinburgh to become a pupil of John Barclay, a well-known anatomist. The lad's ambition was to become a surgeon, and he threw himself whole-heartedly into his anatomical studies. He studied surgery at Edinburgh Royal Infirmary, the London Hospital, and St. Bartholomew's Hospital, becoming a member of both the London and Edinburgh Colleges of Surgeons in 1818.

For a time Liston acted as demonstrator in Barclay's classes, but in 1819 he and his friend and cousin, James Syme, decided to found a school of anatomy and surgery of their own. This endeavour was hampered by the extreme difficulty of obtaining bodies for dissection in Edinburgh, but in spite of these difficulties, Liston and Syme carried on their school with great success for five years.

Meanwhile Liston acted as a surgical clerk at the Royal Infirmary,

Hugh Owen Thomas (see p. 221).
John Barclay, 1758–1826. M.D.Edin., F.R.C.P.Edin. Lecturer on Anatomy and Surgery at Edinburgh. He was at first a private lecturer but in 1804 was formally recognised by the Royal College of Surgeons of Edinburgh.
James Syme (see p. 215).

attending the wards and out-patient departments and watching operations with the undergraduate students. At the same time he was gaining experience as an operating surgeon in a private capacity. He showed remarkable ability, and his fame spread, especially among the poor of Edinburgh. As he had no official status at the Royal Infirmary, his operations were performed at the homes of his patients, with the able assistance of Syme.

Liston's Bone Forceps

Naturally this state of affairs did not please the surgical staff of the Royal Infirmary, who grew jealous of the young man's reputation. They began a campaign against him which culminated in a letter from the manager of the Royal Infirmary forbidding him to visit there on the grounds that his presence was not compatible with the smooth working of the surgical department. Liston appealed against his dismissal, but he could not get an adequate hearing. As a result, his surgical career was severely hampered for five years (1822–27), and, incidentally, the Royal Infirmary was deprived of the services of a brilliant surgeon.

Liston's Long Splint

During this time of comparative exile, Liston wrote many papers, and in one of them advocated the use of the splint which bears his name.

Another unfortunate incident during this period was Liston's quarrel with Syme. The two men had been devoted friends and colleagues until 1823, but professional rivalry caused an increasing coolness, and finally there was an open breach. There was no reconciliation for nearly a quarter of a century; in fact, when it did come, Liston had but a few months to live.

In 1827 the authorities relented, and appointed Liston surgeon to the Royal Infirmary. In 1833, however, Syme defeated him in a contest for the Chair of Clinical Surgery at the University of Edinburgh, and when the Professorship of Surgery at University College, London, became vacant in 1834, Liston applied for the post and obtained it. He was also appointed surgeon to the North London (later University College) Hospital. In London he was received with great enthusiasm, and speedily built up a large private practice.

It is an interesting fact that the first major operation to be performed under ether anaesthesia in England was at University

The operating table upon which Liston performed the first operation under ether in Europe. Note the holes for ropes used to restrain the patient in pre-anaesthetic days

College Hospital by Liston on December 21st 1846. This was a mid-thigh amputation. The patient was Frederick Churchill, a butler, suffering from osteomyelitis of the tibia following a severe injury. After it was over, Liston turned to the crowded audience and said 'This Yankee dodge, gentlemen, beats Mesmerism hollow'. Churchill made a complete recovery.

'A tall man, powerful in form, dressed in a dark bottle-green coat with velvet collar, double-breasted shawl vest, grey trousers, and Wellington boots, the thumb of one hand stuck in the armhole of his vest, comes along in an easy-going way, chewing an orange-wood tooth pick.' That was the description of Robert Liston by a contemporary. His manner, except to his patients, was brusque and rough, and it has been said that he 'was a teacher more by what he did than by what he said.' He was a brilliant and very rapid operator, the latter attribute being of fundamental importance before the days of anaesthesia. He was wont to instruct his assistants to stand, stop-watch in hand, and time him while he performed a major operation.

Liston was very fond of outdoor sports, and up to three months before his death rode to hounds 'like Nimrod.'

He died suddenly on 7th December, 1847, at the age of 53, as the result of an aneurysm of the aorta. His grave is in the cemetery on Highgate Hill.

LUDWIG'S ANGINA

WILHELM
FRIEDRICH
VON LUDWIG
1790–1865

Ludwig described his 'Angina' over 120 years ago.

Wilhelm Friedrich von Ludwig was born near Stuttgart, in what was then the Duchy of Württemberg. He was apprenticed to a surgeon and later studied at the University of Tübingen, where he graduated in medicine in 1811.

The University Clinic, University of Tübingen, in Ludwig's day

These were the stormy times of the Napoleonic Wars, and Württemberg had taken arms on the side of France. Its ruler, Frederick II, had joined Napoleon in his campaigns against Prussia, Austria and Russia, and directly young Ludwig qualified he joined the army as assistant surgeon. The following year he was in charge of a field hospital on the Russian front, and after the battle of Vilna he was taken prisoner by the Russians and remained in captivity for two years.

We next hear of him back at Tübingen, where he applied successfully for the Professorial Chair of Surgery and Midwifery. Before taking up his appointment he visited Vienna and other medical centres.

On his return to take up his new duties he was made personal physician to King Frederick. He appears to have combined the offices of Court Physician and Professor of Surgery and Midwifery in the university with signal success.

It was in 1836, 20 years after he had been appointed to the Chair of Surgery, that he made his first contribution to medical literature. This was a paper upon a form of inflammation of the neck. It was

Ludwig's Angina. The brawny swelling beneath the jaw and the oedema of the floor of the mouth are characteristic features of the condition

largely inspired by observations upon no less a personage than Queen Catherine of Württemberg. Three years later another German surgeon, writing on the same subject, named the condition 'Ludwig's Angina.' This clinical entity comprises massive inflammatory swelling in the submandibular region and the floor of the mouth. It is due to a fulminating infection of the tissues surrounding the submandibular salivary gland. Unless rapidly treated the patient may die from oedema of the glottis. In its earliest stages, the inflammatory swelling may subside on antibiotic treatment. In more advanced cases, a deep incision must be carried out below the mandible and deepened through the mylohyoid muscles to decompress the tissues in the floor of the mouth. Ludwig made practically no other contribution to medical or surgical literature, but his name lives on in this one clinical observation.

The last years of his life were overshadowed by the double affliction of cataract and stone. When he died in 1865 he left the greater part of his large fortune to found a hospital for the poor in Württemberg. This was opened in 1874 for 50 patients, and has since been greatly enlarged.

LUGOL'S
SOLUTION

JEAN
GUILLAUME
AUGUSTE
LUGOL
1786–1851

Jean Guillaume Auguste Lugol was born on 10th August, 1786, at Montauban, Tarn-en-Garonne. He graduated M.D. Paris in 1812, and seven years later was appointed to the staff of the Hôpital St. Louis.

At Paris he gave courses of lectures on pathology, but the great

Charles II touching for the 'King's Evil.'

152

interest of his life was the study of the condition known in his day as scrofula—a collective term applied to tuberculous lymph-nodes and tuberculous bones and joints before it was known that these conditions were caused by the same organism as that which caused pulmonary tuberculosis (see p. 120).

Scrofula has a most interesting history. It is the disease known for centuries as the 'King's Evil', because it was believed that anointed monarchs could cure sufferers from the malady by touching them. It is said that between 1662 and 1682 Charles II 'touched' over 92,000 sufferers from the King's Evil. Every person touched was given a gold coin.

Touchpiece of Charles II (gold) (Raymond Crawfurd)

Lugol's first 'Memoir on the Use of Iodine in Scrofulous Diseases' was read before the Royal Academy of Sciences of Paris in 1829. His treatment comprised fresh air, exercise, cold bathing and drugs. Above all, he placed his faith in iodine therapy. His aqueous solution of iodine (liquor iodidi aquos) for oral administration consists of 5 per cent of iodine, 10 per cent of potassium iodide and distilled water to make 100.

Lugol's solution is not now considered to be of any value in the treatment of tuberculous conditions. At the present time this solution is used mainly in the pre-operative treatment of thyrotoxicosis (Graves's Disease), its value in this respect being pointed out by Dr. H. S. Plummer in 1924.

Lugol's works were translated into English in 1831 and at that

Robert Graves (see p. 88).
Henry S. Plummer, 1874–1936. Physician, Mayo Clinic, Rochester, U.S.A.

time attracted much attention. He made no other outstanding contribution to medicine, and died at Geneva on 16th September, 1851. His laborious researches on scrofula are now forgotten, but his solution keeps his memory alive.

McBURNEY'S POINT

CHARLES McBURNEY 1845-1913

Charles McBurney was one of that brilliant band of surgeons who laid the foundations of the knowledge of acute appendicitis. It was Reginald Fitz who first established the true nature of the disease, coined the term 'appendicitis' and, as a physician, advised his surgical colleagues that 'urgent symptoms demand immediate exposure of the perforated appendix . . . and its treatment according to surgical principles'. Following Fitz's epoch-making paper of 1886, several American surgeons made further contributions to the diagnosis and treatment of this 'new' disease; McBurney was one of the most prominent of these pioneers. He described the point of maximum tenderness in acute appendicitis in the *New York Medical*

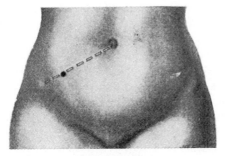

McBurney's Point

Reginald Heber Fitz, 1843-1913. Physician to the Massachusetts General Hospital, Boston.

Journal in 1889. His instructions are explicit. 'It should,' he said, 'be *determined by pressure of one finger*, and the point lies 1½ in. from the anterior superior iliac spine on a straight line drawn from that process to the umbilicus.'

McBurney's muscle-splitting or grid-iron incision for appendicectomy was first described in 1894. He claimed that it gave a more direct approach to the vermiform appendix and that it reduced the incidence of post-operative incisional hernia. Time has proved the truth of both these assertions, and today the grid-iron incision is employed for appendicectomy more often than any other incision.

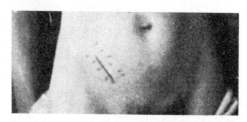

The scar of McBurney's incision for appendicectomy

At the present time in the world there must be hundreds of thousands of individuals who bear the scar of a McBurney's incision on the right lower quadrant of the abdomen. To them, and to their surgeons, McBurney is indeed a name that must not be allowed to wither.

Charles McBurney was born in Roxbury, Massachusetts. He received the benefits of a splendid education. Graduating in Arts from the University of Harvard in 1886, he proceeded to New York and obtained the M.D. degree from the College of Physicians and Surgeons of New York City in 1870. After two years post-graduate study in Europe he commenced practice in New York in 1873. Soon afterwards, at the age of 28, he was appointed assistant demonstrator of anatomy at the College of Physicians and Surgeons. McBurney was elected assistant surgeon to the Bellevue Hospital in 1880, and in 1888, at the age of 43, he was appointed Surgeon-in-Chief at the Roosevelt Hospital. It was not long before this hospital became the Mecca of surgeons from all parts of the world.

Charles McBurney was a surgeon of outstanding ability, and was recognised as one of the leading abdominal surgeons of his day. He published more than 100 papers on surgical subjects, but there is

The Roosevelt Hospital, New York

no doubt that his chief claim to fame is his description of McBurney's point.

McBurney was a fine handsome man. He was devoted to outdoor sports, and was an expert shot and salmon fisherman. At the age of 68 he died suddenly of coronary thrombosis while on a hunting trip.

THE MALPIGHIAN BODIES

The Malpighian Layer of the Skin

MARCELLO
MALPIGHI
1628–1694

When we speak of the Malpighian bodies—the small bodies that can be seen with the naked eye on sectioning the kidney, consisting of an envelope containing terminal globular plexuses and a network of blood-vessels around the commencement of the uriniferous tubules—we commemorate the name of Marcello Malpighi, the founder of microscopical anatomy.

BRANCH OF RENAL ARTERY

URINIFEROUS
TUBULE

BRANCH OF
RENAL VEIN

A Malpighian Body

In addition to his work on the kidney, Malpighi described for the first time the minute structure of scores of organs and tissues of the body. In 1660 Malpighi described the capillaries, thus making Harvey's epoch-making discovery of the circulation of the blood complete. It can be said that he lighted a torch of knowledge that has never been extinguished.

Statue of Malpighi in the University
of Bologna

Marcello Malpighi was born near Bologna. He studied at the famous university near his birthplace, and qualified in medicine when he was 25 years of age. He must have been a young man of outstanding merit, for within three years he obtained a professorship at his own university. He had hardly taken up his duties when he was invited to fill the Chair of Physic at Pisa. This he accepted.

Malpighi was not strong and he found that the climate of Pisa affected his health adversely; consequently at the end of three years he returned to Bologna. Back at the city of his birth he taught and worked in an extramural capacity for some years. Finding, however, that following his resignation all doors of the University were now

William Harvey, 1578–1657. Physician, St. Bartholomew's Hospital, London, Physician to James I and Charles I.

closed to him in his beloved Bologna, he acceded to an offer to fill the Chair of Physic at Messina. None the less, history repeated itself and after a few years he found the post so displeasing that in spite of all efforts to retain him, he insisted on returning once more to Bologna. He remained at Bologna until 1691 when he accepted a summons from Pope Innocent XII to become Physician-in-Chief and Chamberlain at the Papal Court in Rome.

Malpighi himself appears to have been an attractive personality. He was certainly beloved by his pupils and respected by his contemporaries. This did not prevent him becoming involved in bitter quarrels. In one particular feud between his family and a neighbouring clan his nephew was killed. The particular interest to posterity of these circumstances is that during one of the periodic quarrels the original manuscript of years of histological observations was wantonly destroyed by a malicious relative.

Malpighi and his work were early recognised in England. He was elected a Fellow of the Royal Society, and as early as 1687 a complete edition of his writings was published in London.

In addition to the Malpighian bodies, Malpighi's name is today associated with the rete mucosum or Malpighian layer of the skin

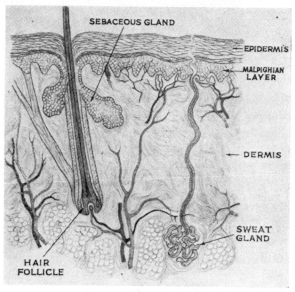

Microscopical section of skin

Malpighi's
Microscope

(the basal layer of the epidermis). It was he, too, who proved that the papillae of the tongue are organs of taste. Indeed there is hardly a tissue in the body which escaped the microscopical scrutiny of Malpighi's seeing eye. This master's work is all the more wonderful when it is realised that he had at his disposal only a primitive microscope but little better than the original model invented by his contemporary, Leeuwenhoek. Truly Malpighi earned the name of the Father of Histology.

Antonj van Leeuwenhoek, 1632–1723, a draper of Delft, in Holland. He devoted his leisure to microscopical studies, grinding his own lens and constructing his own instruments. The most powerful of the 26 microscopes, which Leeuenhoek bequeathed to the Royal Society, had a magnifying power of 160. After his daughter's death, in 1745, the rest of his microscopes were sold, and among them was one the magnifying power of which was no less than 270.

MAYO'S OPERATION FOR
UMBILICAL HERNIA
MAYO'S KIDNEY INCISION
MAYO'S SCISSORS

Dr. Charles H. Mayo   Dr. William J. Mayo
Dr. William W. Mayo

THE MAYO BROTHERS
WILLIAM JAMES MAYO 1861–1939
CHARLES HORACE MAYO 1865–1939

The story of the Mayos and of the Mayo Clinic begins in the year
1845, when William Worrall Mayo, the father of the two famous
brothers, emigrated from Salford, then a village outside Manches-
ter, to the United States of America. The elder Mayo at first
practised his profession of pharmaceutical chemistry in New York
City, but soon turned to the study of medicine. After taking his
M.D. degree in 1854, he worked in various cities until the
opportunities afforded by the development of the North-West
territories induced him to settle in Rochester, Minnesota. In 1862
Dr. Mayo was one of the leaders sent out by the Government to
quell a rising of the Sioux Indians. Still preserved in the Mayo
Clinic is the skeleton of a Sioux chief named Cut Nose, from whose
bones Mayo's sons were taught osteology.

162

William Mayo was born in 1861 and his brother, Charles, in 1865. The two boys helped their father in his busy practice. In after years they were wont to recount how Charles used to stand on a biscuit box in order to assist his father at operations. Long before the boys entered their formal training as medical students they had been receiving practical instruction in Medicine and Surgery from their father. William graduated at the University of Minnesota in 1883, and Charles at the Northwestern University, Chicago, in 1885.

In August, 1883, when a cyclone passed over Rochester, leaving death and destruction in its wake, Dr. William Mayo, Senior, was appointed to take charge of an improvised hospital. So efficient was this emergency hospital that it was suggested to Dr. Mayo he should establish a permanent hospital in Rochester. In 1889, therefore, Dr. Mayo, then aged 70, and his two sons, opened St. Mary's Hospital, with 13 patients and five nurses from the Roman Catholic Sisterhood of St. Francis.

This was the beginning of the Mayo Clinic, now a 'Medical Mecca.' Today the whole town of Rochester is given over to the pursuit of medicine. The high standard first set has been maintained

The Mayo Clinic

by the successive teams of young men trained by the founders. Healing and research go hand in hand, and every resource of science is made available in the fight against disease. At the Mayo Clinic the doctor to whom the patient is first sent conducts the initial examination in his office (as the Americans call the consulting-room), but he has the advantage, when necessary, of being able to utilise the services of one or more of a large number of specialists who also have their offices and laboratories in the same building, and the fee charged is an inclusive one. When in-patient treatment is required the patient can be admitted into one of the hospitals associated with the Clinic.

The Mayo brothers were the soul of the clinic. In other hands the vast organisation might have become as mechanical and unhuman as a motor-car factory, but they preserved the human element. 'Dr. Charlie' and 'Dr. Will' had the humility and humanity that goes with real greatness.

In 1917 the brothers established and endowed the Mayo Foundation for Medical Education and Research to ensure that their work should always be carried on.

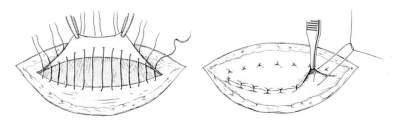

Steps in the overlap operation for umbilical hernia

The greatest debt of surgery to the Mayos is in the ideals, principles and methods they have left behind them. Nevertheless their individual contributions to surgery covered the widest range, and they were both in the very front rank as clinicians and operators. The name of W. J. Mayo will always be associated with the surgery of the stomach and duodenum. He also described his overlap operation for umbilical hernia in 1901 and his L-shaped loin incision for exposure of the kidney in 1912. Charles Mayo's name is attached particularly to the surgery of the thyroid gland. But there was no end to their versatility, and together they wrote more than one thousand papers on surgical subjects. The Mayos, in addition to making contributions to almost every branch of surgery, perfected a number of surgical instruments. Every theatre nurse is familiar with Mayo's scissors.

Mayo's Scissors

One of the most attractive things about the Mayo brothers was the love and respect they had for each other. They lived and worked together as one, in perfect harmony; and in their death they were not divided. Dr. Charlie died of pneumonia in May 1939; Dr. Will died only two months later, of carcinoma of the stomach—a disease whose treatment he had pioneered.

MECKEL'S DIVERTICULUM

JOHANN
FRIEDRICH
MECKEL,
THE YOUNGER
1781–1833

Diverticula of the intestine must have been observed from time to time by anatomists from the earliest times, but it was not until 1810, when Johann Friedrich Meckel, the Younger, wrote an exhaustive paper on this subject that their significance was appreciated, or even that their occasional presence in the human body was recorded. For generations the mnemonic that Meckel's—the principal and only named diverticulum of the intestine—is situated 60 cm proximal to the ileocaecal valve, is 5 cm long, and occurs in 2 per cent of cases, has been taught in every medical school in the world; but useful as these figures are for qualifying examination purposes, they are misleading and inaccurate for surgeons, who must search for a Meckel's diverticulum at operation when a

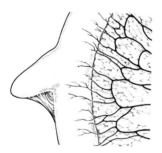

Meckel's diverticulum

perforated inflamed Meckel's diverticulum is the possible cause of peritonitis, the vermiform appendix having been found to be non-culpable. The diverticulum may, in fact, vary in length from 1 to 26 cm in length and be found anywhere from 15 to 160 cm from the ileocaecal valve. Consequently it is unsafe to pronounce that the diverticulum is absent unless the last 150 cm of the ileum has been inspected. It was Meckel who showed that this diverticulum represents failure of the vitelline duct to obliterate—a process that normally occurs during the 7th week of foetal life.

His grandfather, Johann Friedrich Meckel (1714–1774) was Professor of Anatomy, Botany, and Obstetrics in Berlin, and it was he who first described the sphenopalatine (Meckel's) ganglion and the dural space in which the Gasserian ganglion lies (Meckel's cave).

His father, Philip Friedrich Meckel (1756–1803) was Professor of Anatomy and Surgery at Halle, while

His younger brother, August Albert Meckel (1790–1829) held the Chair of Anatomy and Forensic Medicine at Berne, Switzerland.

Johann Friedrich Meckel, the Younger, was born at Halle.

He studied medicine at Halle, Göttingen, Würzburg and Vienna, and graduated M.D. at the university of his native city in 1802.

Young Meckel went on a long study tour through Holland, France, Italy and England, and did not return to Halle until 1806. In 1808 he succeeded his father in the Chair of Anatomy and Surgery at Halle, and out-distanced in fame all the other eminent members of his family, including his paternal grandfather, whose name he bore.

The younger Meckel was a distinguished pathologist and one of the greatest comparative anatomists that Germany has ever produced. His name is known in this field as the discoverer of the first branchial cartilage, known as Meckel's cartilage. The mandible develops around this cartilage, which largely disappears, except for its dorsal end which forms the malleus—one of the ossicles of the middle ear. He has been called the German Cuvier.

Meckel wrote much, his more important works being his treatises on pathological anatomy, normal human anatomy, an atlas of human abnormalities and, his greatest achievement, his system of comparative anatomy. He collected a vast number of specimens for the museum at Halle. This museum was begun by his grandfather and added to by his father, and under Meckel the Younger's care it became one of the finest collections of anatomical and pathological specimens in the world.

Johann Laurentius Gasser. Professor of Anatomy, Vienna, 1723–1765.

Baron Georges Léopold Chrétien Frédéric Dagobert Cuvier, 1769–1832. Lecturer in Comparative Anatomy, University of Paris.

MENIÈRE'S DISEASE

PROSPER MENIÈRE
1799–1862

In 1861, on what proved to be his death-bed, Prosper Menière, Director of the Paris Institution for Deaf-Mutes, described an affection characterised by sudden attacks of deafness, noises in the ear, pallor, nausea and giddiness. The onset usually occurs between 40 and 60 years of age. In about a quarter of cases the opposite ear later becomes affected. The disease is associated with distension of the membranous labyrinth due to increased endolymphatic pressure, but the underlying cause remains unknown. A brilliant scholar and a well-known otologist of his day, Menière died shortly after this epoch-making paper, which was to perpetuate his name, had appeared.

Menière was born at Angers, on the Loire, the third of four children of a tradesman. He received his early education at the Lycée of his native town, and went to Paris to study for the medical profession in 1819. His student career was a brilliant one. He was awarded a Gold Medal in 1826, and obtained his M.D. in 1828. He was acting as clinical assistant to Baron Dupuytren at the Hôtel Dieu, at the time of the political troubles of July and August, 1830, when more than 2,000 wounded rioters were admitted to the hospitals of Paris in one day. Menière wrote a vivid account of his experiences in the casualty department of the Hôtel Dieu, and later this was published in book form.

In 1832 Menière was appointed assistant professor in the Paris faculty of medicine, but his career was interrupted in an unexpected manner. At the suggestion of a friend who was an eminent medicolegal expert, Menière was nominated by the government of King Louis Philippe to ascertain whether the Duchesse de Berry was pregnant. The Duchess, who was the widow of the murdered Duc de Berry, son of Charles X of France, had landed near Marseilles in April, 1832, in an attempt to secure the throne for her 11-year-old son. Her followers were defeated by the government forces and the Duchess herself was captured and imprisoned in the castle of Blays. Menière found that the Duchess was pregnant, and in due course she gave birth to a daughter, the fruit of a secret marriage to an Italian nobleman. The discovery of this marriage and the arrival of the baby deprived the Duchess of the sympathies of her supporters. No longer an object of fear to the French government, she was released and Menière accompanied her to Naples.

Upon his return to Paris Menière acted for a short time as assistant to Professor Chomel.

In 1835 he was sent to the departments of Aude and Haute-Garonne to supervise measures for the prevention of cholera, which was epidemic at that time. In 1837 he applied for the vacant professorship of medicine and hygiene, writing a brilliant thesis on clothing and cosmetics. He was unsuccessful, but in the following year he secured the appointment of physician-in-chief to the Institution for Deaf-Mutes.

Henceforth his professional work lay almost entirely in the field of otology.

Menière was a well-known figure in the intellectual world of Paris, and was intimate with Balzac, Victor Hugo and other great writers as well as with the leading medical men. He was himself a highly cultured man and his life-long study of the Greek and Latin classics was responsible for two learned volumes on *Medical Studies on the Latin Poets* and on *Cicero as a Physician*.

Menière married in 1838 Mlle. Becquerel, a member of the same family as Antoine Becquerel, the discoverer of radioactivity. Their son, Dr. Emile Menière, was also a noted otologist. Prosper Menière died on 7th February, 1862, of influenzal pneumonia.

Auguste François Chomel, 1788–1858. Professor of Clinical Medicine and Physician to the Hôtel Dieu, Paris.

Honoré de Balzac, 1799–1850. Famous French novelist. Author of over 80 books depicting every phase and aspect of French life.

Victor Hugo, 1802–1885. Famous French dramatist and novelist. Author of world-renowned classics such as Les Miserables.

Marcus Tullius Cicero, 106–43 B.C. A great Roman orator and philosopher.

Antoine Henri Becquerel, 1852–1908. Professor of Physics at the École Polytechnique, Paris. In 1903 he was awarded the Nobel Prize for Physics jointly with Pierre and Marie Curie.

MOYNIHAN'S GALL-BLADDER FORCEPS

MOYNIHAN'S GUTTER

LORD MOYNIHAN 1865–1936

Berkeley George Andrew Moynihan came of Irish stock. His father, Andrew, was a remarkable man who won the Victoria Cross in the Crimean War; as a sergeant he killed five Russians and rescued two officers under fire during an attack on the Redan. Most unusually in those days, he was commissioned from the ranks and eventually became a Captain, only to die in Malta of Malta fever when Berkeley was only a year old. The future surgeon was taken by his mother back to her parents in Leeds. As time went on he became a 'blue-coat' boy, a pupil at that famous school, Christ's Hospital. His first intention was to follow the family tradition and enter the Army or Navy, but he changed his mind and decided to study medicine.

Leeds was at that time, and still is, one of the leading provincial centres of surgery. Moynihan carried all before him in his student career. He qualified in 1887, obtained the F.R.C.S. in 1890, and was awarded a gold medal in the examination for the M.S. London. Following qualification he held the posts of house surgeon and resident surgical officer in the General Infirmary at Leeds concurrently. In 1895, at the age of 30, he married the daughter of the Leeds surgeon T. R. Jessop, and in 1896 he was appointed Assistant Surgeon to the General Infirmary.

Thomas Richard Jessop, 1837–1903. Surgeon, General Infirmary at Leeds.

170

During these early years of his surgical career Moynihan came in daily contact with Mayo Robson, one of the foremost British pioneers in abdominal surgery, and there can be little doubt that Mayo Robson was largely if not entirely responsible for laying the foundations of what proved to be an exceptionally brilliant career.

Following in the footsteps of his teacher, Moynihan began to publish careful observations on diseases of the stomach, biliary passages, intestines and pancreas, and to put forward suggestions for improving the technique of abdominal operations. In 1901 appeared a book on *Diseases of the Stomach*, written jointly with Mayo Robson.

Moynihan's growing reputation afforded him wonderful opportunities for developing special experience in the comparatively new field of abdominal surgery. He made full use of these opportunities.

Moynihan's Gall-bladder Forceps

In 1904 appeared the first edition of his text-book on *Abdominal Operations*, a work which made his name known to surgeons on both sides of the Atlantic.

In 1904 also it was Moynihan who first made use of the term 'hunger pain'—pain eased by the taking of food, and appearing two to four hours after a meal, in cases of duodenal ulcer.

Moynihan was a wonderful exponent of gentle, unhurried, but purposeful surgical craftsmanship. He combined this with refinements in aseptic technique and so evolved the new standards required for successful operations upon intraperitoneal organs. No surgeon could have put more of his heart and soul into perfecting his technique than did Moynihan. Operating was to him a 'ritual, a sacred rite and an art.' His viewpoint can be caught by reading these words of his: 'There is nothing in the craft of any art so

Sir Arthur William Mayo Robson, 1853–1933. Professor of Surgery and Surgeon to the General Infirmary at Leeds.

exquisitely beautiful that it can surpass that shown by the skilful master of surgery.'

Such an artist was Moynihan. On one occasion the celebrated J. B. Murphy, a hard critic, was present in the operating theatre at Leeds watching Moynihan perform. Murphy whispered to a friend that he would have travelled from America with the one object of witnessing such perfection. On another occasion a French visitor, after watching Moynihan's meticulous haemostasis, is reported to have remarked, 'Is then your English blood so precious?'

While we have emphasised the greatness of Moynihan as operator (probably he did more to refine surgical technique than any other British surgeon), it must not be lost sight of that he was an accomplished diagnostician and he never ceased to stress the importance of physiology and of what he termed the 'pathology of the living.'

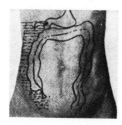

Moynihan's Gutter.
When a duodenal ulcer
perforates, sometimes the
ascending colon acts as a watershed, and directs the escaping
contents to the right iliac fossa,
and the symptoms and signs
simulate those of acute
appendicitis

He had remarkable descriptive powers. He noted how the right paracolic gutter may allow fluid from a perforated duodenal ulcer to track into the right iliac fossa ('Moynihan's gutter'). He gave the vivid name of 'strawberry gall bladder' to the condition of cholesterosis, when the little yellow flecks of cholesterol stand out against the reddened mucosa of the gall bladder.

He was created Baron Moynihan of Leeds in 1929, when until then the only other surgeon to have been elevated to the peerage was Lister.

By virtue of his commanding personality, he was instrumental in causing the surgical profession as a whole to take notice of a number of advances that could be applied to surgery in general and abdominal surgery in particular. The creation of the Association of

Lord Lister (see p. 139).
John B. Murphy (see p. 174).

Surgeons of Great Britain and Ireland and the launching of the *British Journal of Surgery*, in 1915, were in a large measure due to his drive and imagination.

As a public orator Lord Moynihan had few equals. His more formal orations and addresses were prepared with meticulous care

The General Infirmary at Leeds

and were delivered without notes and without hesitation. Audiences hung upon his honeyed words, and his speeches never failed to produce a profound effect.

Lord Moynihan was always interested in politics and his name was mentioned for several high offices, including that of Ambassador to the United States.

At the age of 71 years Lord Moynihan died at his house, Carr Manor, Leeds, on 7th September, 1936, one week after the death of Lady Moynihan. An offer to be buried in Westminster Abbey was refused by his family.

MURPHY'S SIGN
MURPHY'S DRIP
MURPHY'S BUTTON

JOHN
BENJAMIN
MURPHY*
1857–1916

John B. Murphy was born on a farm near Appleton, Wisconsin. His parents were emigrants from Ireland. He studied medicine at Rush Medical College, Chicago, and graduated M.D. in 1879. After holding an internship at Cook County Hospital, he spent two years in post-graduate study in Vienna under Billroth. Returning to Chicago, he was appointed lecturer in surgery at Rush Medical College, subsequently becoming professor. He was also at one time professor of surgery in the Northwestern University Medical School, and attending surgeon at Cook County Hospital. In 1895 he became chief of the surgical staff of the Mercy Hospital, which position he held until his death. The Mercy Hospital was the scene of his greatest triumphs.

Murphy advanced surgical knowledge of almost every region of the body. He was one of the first to investigate the cause and treatment of peritonitis following appendicitis. He devoted much attention to the surgery of the lung, and is rightly regarded as one of the pioneers of thoracic surgery. Independently of Forlanini, the Italian, he suggested artificial pneumothorax, and he was the first surgeon in America to carry out this procedure.

In 1897 Murphy introduced end-to-end suture of blood-vessels

---

* John B. Murphy was christened plain John Murphy, but when he went to school he noticed that the majority of the other boys had at least two initials and so, determined not to be inferior, he added the 'B.'

Theodor Billroth (see p. 18).
Carlo Forlanini, 1847–1918. Director, Medical Clinic, Pavia.

and performed the first successful suture of a divided femoral artery. Towards the end of his life Murphy devoted himself largely to the surgery of bones and joints. He advocated bone-grafting in cases of ununited fracture and he inserted a living graft of fascia between the bone ends of excised joints to restore movement after ankylosis. Murphy's work on the surgery of the nervous system helped to lay the foundation for extensive developments in this direction.

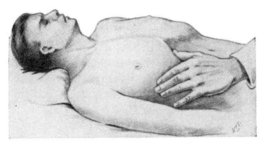

Murphy's sign

His name lives for some of his relatively minor achievements:

Murphy's sign of the presence of cholecystitis is a standard method of physical examination when this condition is suspected.

If continuous gentle pressure is exerted over the right hypochondrium while the patient takes a deep breath, there is a 'catch in the breath' just before the zenith of the inspiration, i.e. as the edge of the liver descends below the costal margin and the fundus of the tender gall-bladder becomes subjected to pressure.

Murphy's 'Drip.' Murphy initiated the continuous method of giving saline solution per rectum (proctoclysis).

Actually there was no drip in Murphy's apparatus. Murphy emphasised that the height of the reservoir should not be more than one foot above the rectum, that the delivery tube should be of comparatively wide calibre, and that his glass bulb with many perforations should always be employed. Murphy's apparatus is not intercepted by any form of dripper. Consequently, flatus can be expelled through the wide calibre tube into the reservoir.

Murphy's 'kidney punch' is a much used clinical sign for eliciting tenderness of a kidney not otherwise apparent because of the deep, well-protected situation of the kidneys.

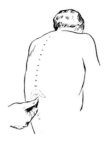

Murphy's Kidney Punch   Murphy's Button

Murphy's Button. That ingenious device for effecting intestinal anastomosis, after a short-lived, world-wide trial, was relegated to the museum. Nevertheless, it was this invention which demonstrated that intestine could be successfully anastomosed after resection, thus paving the way to modern surgical achievement in this direction.

Perhaps the greatest of Murphy's triumphs was his success as a clinical teacher. In spite of his high, shrill voice, his eloquence and force of personality held his audience spell-bound. A glance at the accompanying photograph, which portrays a typical demonstration at the Murphy Clinic in 1913, will leave the reader in no doubt as to his immense following.

Murphy was a tall and powerfully built man, with a florid complexion, a short red beard, parted carefully in the middle, and a red moustache. His rise was meteoric. He overcame the handicaps of early impecuniosity (his widowed mother was without means), bouts of ill-health (he came from stock riddled with tuberculosis), and, what was probably for him the most difficult, the hurdles of unbridled jealousy erected by his professional brethren. He rose, as was inevitable—enthusiasm, energy and signal ability such as his could not be suppressed. Nevertheless, it is unlikely that he would have reached the glittering heights he attained without especial favours. His charming and accomplished wife not only entered into and helped him in every aspect of his professional life, but she exercised a brake upon his highly geared mechanism, which, at times, was inclined to race.

Murphy practised in a city that was developing so rapidly as to take a place among the largest in the world. He lived in an era of peace and plenty, and at a time when, by reason of radiology,

John B. Murphy's Clinic at the Mercy Hospital

bacteriology and biochemistry, diagnosis was becoming more and more accurate; above all, he embarked upon his career in the 'Golden Age' of surgery when by reason of asepsis and better anaesthesia regions of the body hitherto considered closed forever to the surgeon were being exposed to the light of day.

The Cook County Hospital, Chicago. The largest general hospital in the world. It contains 3,400 beds. In the early '90s J. B. Murphy was on the surgical staff

Murphy had several minor attacks of coronary thrombosis, and at the age of 59 years he succumbed to a major attack of this disease, which is so prevalent among those professional men who work at high pressure.

In addition to being a man with superabundant energy, John B. Murphy was activated by very high ideals, which can be summarised in his own words, 'The patient is the centre of the medical universe, around which all our works revolve and towards which all our efforts tend'.

PAGET'S DISEASE
OF NIPPLE

PAGET'S DISEASE
OF BONE

SIR JAMES
PAGET
1814–1899

Sir James Paget was one of the Great Victorians. Eminent as a physiologist, pathologist, surgeon and teacher, his nobility of character and his incessant application to duty made him a leader of the profession in that age of great men.

James Paget was born at Yarmouth, the youngest of the nine surviving children of the 17 born to Samuel and Sarah Paget. His father was a brewer and ship-owner. James attended a private school in Yarmouth, and at the age of 16 was apprenticed to a surgeon on the staff of the local hospital. During his apprenticeship Paget, with an elder brother as co-author, wrote a book on the natural history of Great Yarmouth. At the age of 20 Paget enrolled as a medical student at St. Bartholomew's Hospital, London, and in the following year, while dissecting, he observed tiny gritty areas in the muscles of a subject. Paget examined these under a microscope, and made original sketches of the parasite that was revealed; these sketches are preserved in the library of the Royal College of Surgeons. The preparations were examined by Richard (later Sir Richard) Owen, who named the worm *Trichina spiralis*, and took the credit for the discovery.

James Paget's father, as a consequence of financial reverses, was unable to pay the necessary 'dressing fee' to the surgeons of the hospital. As a result, Paget never became a surgical dresser, but had to be satisfied with acting as a clinical clerk to the physicians, who required no such fee. Nevertheless, at the age of 22 he passed the examination for the M.R.C.S. (Eng.).

Sir Richard Owen, 1804–1892. K.C.B., F.R.C.S. (Eng.), F.R.S. Hunterian Professor of Comparative Anatomy at the Royal College of Surgeons, and later Keeper of the National History Collection of the British Museum.

It was vital for Paget to earn his own living directly he qualified, and this he did by teaching and acting as sub-editor of the *London Medical Gazette*.

In 1837 Paget was appointed Curator of the Museum at St. Bartholomew's Hospital, and a little later Demonstrator of Morbid Anatomy as well. At the age of 27 he was elected Warden of the College for Resident Students, then newly opened in connection with St. Bartholomew's Hospital. This post he retained for eight years. During this time he made a complete descriptive index of all the anatomical and pathological specimens in the museum of the hospital.

In 1847 a vacancy occurred for the post of assistant surgeon to the hospital, for which, of course, Paget applied. The fact that he had neither acted as a surgical dresser nor as a house-surgeon was moved by the opposition as a factor to bar his candidature; this, however, was over-ruled, and he came out top of the poll.

Paget's Disease of Bone

Paget was an indefatigable worker who proved himself to be an exceptional clinical observer. He was an admirable teacher, an eloquent lecturer, and a sound, but not a brilliant, operator.

He is now chiefly remembered by reason of his original description of Paget's disease of bone (osteitis deformans) and Paget's disease of the nipple. In an article in the St. Bartholomew's Reports for 1874 he described 15 cases of disease of the nipple, all of which were followed by cancer in the substance of the underlying mammary gland. Two years later he read a paper before the Royal Medico-Chirurgical Society 'On a form of chronic inflammation of

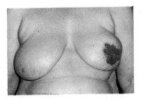

Paget's Disease of Nipple

the bones' and in 1882 described seven further cases before the same Society.

The thickening and bowing of the long bones of the legs, the enlargement of the skull, requiring progressively larger hats, the slowly developing curvature and rigidity of the spine were accurately described, together with the post mortem appearances. In one patient cancerous change had taken place in the left radius and in the skull vault.

Amidst an extraordinary busy life (for, in addition to his hospital work, he was building up what was to be the largest surgical practice in London) he found time to index minutely all the specimens of the Hunterian collection of the Royal College of Surgeons in the same way as he had catalogued the specimens in his own hospital. This task took him seven years. Yet he never appeared unduly hurried, nor was he ever unpunctual in keeping appointments. Of his assistants he expected the same determination of purpose and achievement; to one of his subordinates who complained that he had no time, Paget retorted tersely 'Sir, you have all the time there is.'

In person Paget was slight, a little above medium height, his face rather long, his cheeks somewhat flushed, and his eyes bright. His voice was soft and he spoke fluently. Although his public utterances were delivered with an air of spontaneity, they were most carefully prepared beforehand. As an orator he had few equals, and no less an authority than Mr. Gladstone once said that he divided people into two classes—those who had, and those who had not, heard James Paget. His lectures to students were prepared with the same care as his formal speeches, while his writings are among the classics of medical literature. Having climbed to the highest rung of the surgical ladder in London, honours were showered upon him.

William Ewart Gladstone, 1809–1898. The great Liberal statesman, who was Prime Minister of England three times.

He was elected F.R.S. (1851) and appointed Surgeon Extraordinary to Queen Victoria (1858). On resigning from the active staff of St. Bartholomew's in 1871 he was created a baronet. In 1875 he was President of the College of Surgeons, and in the next year became Serjeant Surgeon to the Queen.

Sir James Paget always worked at the highest pressure, 'to within an inch of his life' as he once said. When he gave up operating at the age of 64, he continued in consulting practice, and was incessantly active in public duties and at medical societies. When 77 he travelled to Rome to see a patient, and in his eightieth year gave an address before the Abernethian Society, formed in Abernethy's day, composed of students, graduates and teachers of St. Bartholomew's Hospital for the purpose of scientific discussion, is still in existence.

When over 70 years of age he decided to make use of his vast collection of case-records, and after eight years' work produced, in 1891, his *Studies of Old Case Books*.

He died in his eighty-fifth year, and was buried in Finchley Cemetery after a funeral service at Westminster Abbey.

John Abernethy, 1764–1831. Surgeon, St. Bartholomew's Hospital.

PAUL'S TUBE
PAUL-MIKULICZ OPERATION

FRANK THOMAS PAUL
1851-1941

Paul's tube may be employed as a temporary measure to drain away the faecal matter after a colostomy has been performed, usually for obstruction of the large bowel. It will be noticed that in the original illustration of Paul's tube (which is taken from the *Liverpool Medico-Chirurgical Journal* of 1892) that the glass tube

Paul's Tube

has at one end *two* bevels; it is this end which is inserted into the bowel and the other is connected with the rubber tubing. Around the bevel nearer the angle of the twin bevelled end is tied a purse-string suture, which has been inserted into the coats of the bowel before the opening into the intestine is made. Between the first and second bevels is tied a piece of tape, which makes a water-tight junction between the bowel and the tube.

Frank Thomas Paul was born at Pentney, Norfolk. He received his medical education at Guy's Hospital, qualifying in 1871. He obtained his M.R.C.S., L.R.C.P. in 1873. In 1878 he became a

The Royal Infirmary, Liverpool

Fellow of the Royal College of Surgeons of England. In 1875 he was appointed the first resident medical officer of the Liverpool Royal Infirmary. At this time he describes his hospital work thus: 'Erysipelas, septicaemia, pyaemia and hospital and gas gangrene were rampant. One out of three ovariotomies and excisions of the breast died of sepsis. Most of the surgeons of that time operated in a dirty frock coat.' Paul subsequently was elected surgeon to the Stanley Hospital and the Southern Hospital. Eventually he was appointed surgeon to the Royal Infirmary, Liverpool, where he spent the last 20 years of his hospital career.

In contrast to his early experiences, he says, 'It was a very wonderful twenty years in which the safety of operations increased astoundingly. In my last years I did over a thousand consecutive breast cases without a death, and in appendix cases, with the exclusion of five hopeless cases already suffering from general peritonitis, also one thousand consecutive recoveries.' It is little wonder that Paul acquired a great reputation in Liverpool.

Much of Paul's spare time was devoted to microscopical study. He was an expert at staining and interpreting pathological tissues.

Paul's operation of extra-abdominal resection of a segment of colon for carcinoma of the colon is well known throughout the world. It is frequently referred to as the Paul-Mikulicz operation,

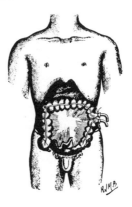

Extra-abdominal resection of a
colonic tumour using Paul's tubes
(Liverpool Med.-Chir. Journal 1903)

but this is hardly justifiable seeing that Paul anticipated Mikulicz
in publishing this technique by no less than 10 years. From an
illustration taken from the *Liverpool Medico-Chirurgical Journal*
of 1903 the principles of the operation that Paul devised can be
seen. The obstructing carcinoma is mobilised, brought outside the
abdominal cavity and resected, the divided ends being brought out
as a double-barrelled colostomy. In Paul's original operation, his
tubes were inserted into the proximal and distal stomas. At a later
stage, the colostomy is closed.

For many years after he had retired from the Royal Infirmary,
Paul was in active practice, being consulting surgeon to the Royal
Infirmary and on the staff of Hoylake Cottage Hospital. In 1925, on
the occasion of his seventy-fifth birthday, he was presented by the

Bronze of Paul's right hand
(Liverpool Medical Institution)

Johann von Mikulicz-Radecki, 1850–1905. Professor of Surgery, Breslau.

surgeons of Liverpool with a volume of papers selected from his most important contributions to surgical and pathological literature. At the same time a bronze cast of his hand was presented to the Liverpool Medical Institution, of which he had been a leading member for over 50 years. In the course of a speech which the late Frank Jeans made on this occasion, he said, 'Paul operating in the heyday of his manual efficiency always made me think that he did with his hands what Pavlova did with her feet.'

Paul retired to Grayshott near Hindhead, where he grew orchids and took colours photographs. Paul's long life of achievement came to an end when he was 90 years of age.

Frank Jeans, 1878–1933. Surgeon, The Royal Infirmary, Liverpool.

POLITZER'S
BAG

ADAM
POLITZER
1835–1920

When Professor Adam Politzer of Vienna died in 1920, at the age of 85 years, he had long been regarded as the father of modern otology. He had laboured at his speciality for more than half a century, and it is probably true to say that no other aural specialist did so much original work or attained such a position of authority as did this little Viennese professor.

Politzer was born in Alberti, Hungary, and received his degree of Doctor of Medicine from the University of Vienna in 1859. Early in his career he became interested in diseases of the ear and he realised the opening there was for this speciality in Vienna. He determined to equip himself thoroughly, and so spent several years travelling over Europe studying acoustics and the anatomy, physiology and pathology of the ear under the most famous masters of the time.

Politzer's Bag

Politzer returned to Vienna in 1861, and he so impressed the authorities with the results of his scientific journeys that a new Chair of Otology was created for him. He had only four pupils in his first course, but it was not long before aurists flocked to his clinic from all parts of the world. He was a model teacher; not only was his knowledge profound, but he could inspire others with his

187

untiring zeal for conscientious work. As many Englishmen and Americans attended his classes, most of his teaching was given in excellent English, but Sir St. Clair Thomson, who visited his clinic in 1893, heard him speak fluently in German, French, Hungarian, Czech and Italian during one lesson.

There is no department of otology to which Professor Politzer did not make fundamental contributions. In 1863 he described his method of inflating the middle ear for diagnostic or therapeutic purposes by means of a soft rubber bag, and Politzer's bag serves to remind us of his discovery.

The Old University Building, Vienna, used until 1884

His favourite field was the anatomy and pathological anatomy of the ear. He was the first to obtain pictures of the tympanic membrane by illumination. Politzer was a talented artist and he excelled in making models in plaster. His evenings were spent with microscope and drawing pencils, working away at his vast collection.

In 1878 appeared the first edition of his *Manual of Diseases of the Ear*, which is without exception the greatest text-book on the subject. Professor Politzer was the author of more than one hundred monographs and articles, and his writings are a mine of information.

Politzer was a neat and dapper little man, with sparkling dark eyes and a musical voice. His genial manner and courteous attitude won for him the esteem of all who visited his clinic.

Sir St. Clair Thomson, 1859–1943. Physician for Diseases of the Throat and Nose, King's College Hospital, London.

POTT'S FRACTURE
POTT'S DISEASE
POTT'S PUFFY
TUMOUR

PERCIVAL
POTT
1714–1788

The house in Threadneedle Street, London, in which Percival Pott
was born was pulled down in 1780, in order to accommodate an
extension of the Bank of England. His father was a scrivener. (A
drafter of documents, particularly legal documents), and died when
Percival was only three years old, leaving his mother with very little
money. They were helped, however, by a wealthy relative who was,
in fact, the Bishop of Rochester, and when the boy was 15 years of
age he was apprenticed for two hundred guineas to Edward Nourse,
then Assistant Surgeon to St. Bartholomew's Hospital.

The Theatre of the Barber's
Hall

Edward Nourse, 1701–1761, F.R.S. Surgeon to St. Bartholomew's Hospital, London.

189

Pott appears to have acquired a reputation early, for before the end of his apprenticeship he moved to a large house in Fenchurch Street, and lived there with his mother and sister. In 1736 he obtained the Grand Diploma of the Barber Surgeons' Company, which corresponded in some respects to the Fellowship of the Royal College of Surgeons at the present time, and was granted only after

A view of St. Bartholomew's Hospital in 1740

a searching examination. It was customary for candidates for the Grand Diploma to call on the Examiners before the examination, but Pott was prevented from doing so by a long confinement case. In spite of this lapse, he passed the examination, which goes to show he was well known and held in esteem by the Company. After the death of his mother, he married and moved to Watling Street, near St. Paul's Cathedral.

In 1744 he was appointed Assistant Surgeon to St. Bartholomew's Hospital, and in 1749 full Surgeon. During this time, he acquired a great reputation as a teacher, his forte being lecture-demonstrations, a form of teaching of which he is said to be the pioneer.

In 1758, while riding in Kent Street, Southwark, now the Old Kent Road, Pott was thrown from his horse, and sustained a compound fracture of the tibia (not, as popularly supposed, a fracture-dislocation of the ankle, Pott's fracture-dislocation, but a fracture of the shaft of the bone). The incident was described by his son-in-law thus: Conscious of the dangers attendant on fractures of this nature and thoroughly aware how much they may be increased by rough treatment or improper position, he would not suffer himself to be moved until he had made the necessary disposition. He sent to Westminster for two chairmen to bring their poles; he patiently lay on the cold pavement, it being the middle of January, until they arrived. In this situation he purchased a door to which he made them nail their poles. When all was ready, he caused himself to be laid on it, and on it was carried home.

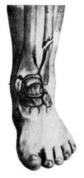

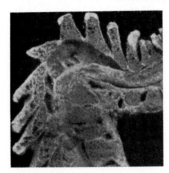

Pott's Fracture Dislocation   Pott's disease of the spine, with gross angular curvature

The distinguished patient was examined by many of his fellow surgeons, who consulted and concurred that the only course was amputation. However, while the instruments were being got ready Edward Nourse, Pott's old teacher, arrived, and on examining the limb decided that it might be possible to save it. The other surgeons deferred to Nourse's opinion, and Pott retained his leg. In due course the wound healed satisfactorily.

While he was confined to the house Pott took to writing, and, to commence with, not unnaturally, he chose the subject of fractures. Later he wrote on many other subjects. Two inflammatory conditions are named after him: Pott's Puffy Tumour, associated with osteomyelitis of a bone of the skull, secondary to frontal sinusitis or to an extradural abscess, and Pott's Disease, or spinal caries due to tuberculosis. It was he who first described chimney sweep's cancer (carcinoma of the scrotum). Percival Pott's lectures became the most celebrated in London, and served to disseminate his views and methods throughout Europe. In 1764, at the age of 50, he was elected a Fellow of the Royal Society.

In 1787 he retired from St. Bartholomew's after having 'served the charity, man and boy, for half a century.' He died in 1788 from pneumonia, and was buried in St. Mary's Aldermary Church, London, where a tablet commemorating him could be seen until recent times.

RAMSTEDT'S OPERATION

CONRAD RAMSTEDT
1867–1963

As a result of post-mortem examinations on two infants who had died of this disease, hypertrophic pyloric stenosis of infants was described by Harald Hirschsprung in 1888. There had been a few earlier descriptions, commencing with Patrick Blair (*Philosophical Transactions*, 1717), but it was Hirschsprung's paper that aroused world-wide interest. In spite of the high mortality of the condition

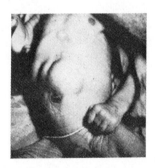

Visible peristalsis in an infant with hypertrophic pyloric stenosis

physicians were reluctant, if not vehemently opposed, to advise operation for its relief. From 1892 to 1912 reports of attempts to relieve the obstruction by various forms of pyloroplasty appeared from time to time; nearly all ended fatally. One notable exception was a patient operated upon by Löbker of Bochum, who employed

Harold Hirschsprung (see p. 101).
Carl Löbker, 1854–1912. Director, Knappschaftskrankenhaus 'Bergmannsheil,' Bochum, Westphalia.

gastrojejunostomy. In 1907 Fredet suggested a new operation in which the serous and muscular coats of the pylorus alone were cut. Fredet's operation and that of Weber (1908) paved the way for Ramstedt's operation, which was described in 1912.

Ramstedt's two successful cases were reported at a Medical Congress held in Münster in 1912, and were published in the *Medizinische Klinik* of 20th October, 1912. The report of the first case reads as follows:

> When in September, 1911 . . . I was first confronted with an operation for pyloric stenosis, I decided to perform the partial pyloroplasty according to Weber. During the operation I noticed, after section of the firmly contracted, almost bloodless and hypertrophied muscular ring, that the wound edges gaped markedly; I had the impression that the stenosis was already overcome. Nevertheless I sutured the incision transversely in order to complete the Weber pyloroplasty. The tension of the wound edges was, however, very great and the sutures cut through so that the union of the wound edges in the opposite direction was incomplete. I therefore covered the sutured area with a tag of omentum for protection.
>
> The child is cured. Today, about one year after the operation, he is developed as well as any child of his age.

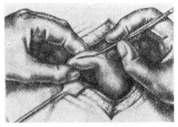

Incising the serous and muscular
coats of the pylorus

The hypertrophied muscle
divided and the mucous
membrane bulging into the
incision

In the second case Ramstedt decided to leave the incision gaping; it was a complete success. The second infant operated on by Ramstedt was the son of a physician, and it is remarkable that nearly all the patients on whom Ramstedt operated for this condition early in his large series were the children of medical men. Since the introduction of the Ramstedt procedure the operative mortality has fallen from 50 per cent to practically zero.

Pierre Fredet, 1870–1946. Surgeon, Pitié and Charité Hospitals, Paris.
Wilhelm Weber, 1872–1928. Surgeon, Dresden.

Conrad Ramstedt, the son of a physician, was born at Hamers-leben, a village in Central Prussia. He attended the gymnasium at Magdeburg and studied medicine at Heidelberg, Berlin and Halle, graduating M.D. Halle in 1894. From 1895 to 1901 he was an assistant in the surgical clinic at Halle, and he then became a military surgeon. He held high rank in the medical department of the German Army during the First World War, and after his discharge in 1919 became chief surgeon to the Rafaelklinik at Münster. Apart from five articles on the surgical treatment of

The Raphael Clinic, Münster. This building was destroyed by bombing during World War II

pyloric stenosis, his main contributions to medical literature are the chapters on the surgery of the male genito-urinary organs which he wrote for the *Handbuch der praktischen Chirurgie* edited by Bergmann. Bruns and Mikulicz (1927).

With regard to the eponym Ramstedt's operation, it should be noted that the name is spelled Rammstedt in the original report. Professor Ramstedt changed his name from Rammstedt to Ramstedt, and this accounts for the two versions. In some textbooks on surgery it is spelt with one 'm'; in most two 'm'. One 'm' is correct.

VON RECKLING-
HAUSEN'S DISEASE

VON RECKLING-
HAUSEN'S DISEASE
OF BONE

FRIEDRICH DANIEL
VON RECKLINGHAUSEN
1833–1910

Friedrich Daniel von Recklinghausen, one of Germany's most distinguished pathologists, was born at Gütersloh, Westphalia. He obtained his M.D. degree at Berlin in 1855 and spent six years as assistant to the world-famous pathologist Rudolf Virchow. In 1865 von Recklinghausen was appointed professor of pathological anatomy at the University of Königsberg. In the following year he accepted the chair at Würzburg, and in 1872 he transferred to Strasbourg, becoming professor of pathology in the newly founded university of that city.

In 1882 von Recklinghausen described neurofibromatosis, although Robert William Smith had written in 1849 a splendid monograph entitled *A Treatise on the Pathology, Diagnosis and Treatment of Neuroma.*

This is a condition of multiple tumours arising from the connective tissue sheaths of cutaneous nerves. The cranial and spinal nerves may also be involved and there is often associated pigmentation of the skin, producing the characteristic 'cafe au lait' stains. Occasionally plexiform neurofibromatosis may affect the fifth cranial nerve, producing pendulous folds of skin; the best known example of this was the 'Elephant Man', whose skeleton can be seen in the Pathology Museum of the London Hospital.

Von Recklinghausen also described the generalised decalcification of the skeleton associated with cyst formation (osteitis fibrosa cystica). The disease had been noted before but had not been studied systematically until Von Recklinghausen's accurate

Rudolf Virchow, 1821–1902. Director of the Pathological Institute of the Charité Hospital, Berlin. He added 23,000 specimens to the museum of this hospital, and is rightly regarded as the Father of Morbid Anatomy.
Robert William Smith, 1807–1873. Professor of Surgery, University of Dublin.

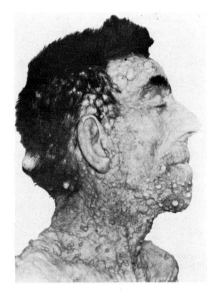

Generalised neurofibromatosis:
von Recklinghausen's disease

Parathyroid tumour exposed

description of three patients in 1891. In 1903 Askanazy found a parathyroid tumour in a patient with this condition and in 1925 Mandl was the first surgeon to remove a parathyroid tumour and to note healing of the bony lesion. The condition is now known to be associated with the presence of a parathyroid functioning adenoma with an elevation of the serum calcium, depression of the serum phosphorus and increased excretion of calcium and phosphorus in the urine. Removal of the parathyroid adenoma is followed by gradual return of the skeleton to normality.

Max Askanazy, 1865–1940. Pathologist, Geneva.
Felix Mandl, 1892–1957. Surgeon, Vienna. Removed a parathyroid tumour from a Viennese tram conductor with osteitis fibrosa cystica, with remarkable improvement.

As might be expected, the attachment of von Recklinghausen's name to two completely different conditions has led to confusion. On this account teachers of surgery have encouraged von Recklinghausen's second clinical entity being designated descriptively, viz. osteitis fibrosa.

The Anatomy and Pathology Institute, University of Strasbourg

Von Recklinghausen left his mark on almost every field of pathology. To quote but a few: he first described fatty and hyaline degeneration of muscles, invented silver impregnation for staining nervous tissue and first recognised basophilic mast cells in the blood. Von Recklinghausen was a man of fine personal character, and had a great reputation as a teacher. He resigned from his professorship in 1906, and died at Strasbourg at the age of 77 years.

REITER'S DISEASE

HANS
REITER
1881–1969

Reiter's disease is characterised by non-gonococcal purulent ureth-ritis followed in two to fourteen days by arthritis and conjunctivitis. The arthritis is very painful, and is punctuated by remissions and exacerbations. The knees, the great toe joints and the interphal-angeal joints are affected most often, but other joints frequently are involved. The conjunctivitis is severe and long-lasting. Compli-cations such as iritis are not uncommon. Intermittent pyrexia, night

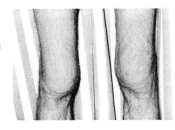

Bilateral knee involvement in Reiter's syndrome

sweats and secondary anaemia are the rule. The disease is con-sidered to be an example of a reactive arthritis, where the joint inflammation is produced in response to changes induced by micro-organisms at a site remote from the joint itself. A familiar example of this is the association between rheumatic fever and the strepto-coccus. Two organisms so far known to be involved in the disease are *Shigella* and *Yersinia enterocolitica* in the gut. *Chlamydia trachomatis* in the genito-urinary tract has also been implicated. There is a strong genetic predisposition in that about three-quarters of patients possess the antigen HLAB27. Treatment with steroidal

199

anti-inflammatory agents is effective although treatment of the microbial infection seems to have no effect on the progress of the disease.

Hans Reiter was born in 1881 in Leipzig, the son of a manufacturer and owner of a factory. After Reiter had matriculated from the Thomas Gymnasium, at the age of 20 he commenced his medical studies in the University of Leipzig, and continued them in Breslau and Tübingen. In 1906 he graduated M.D. Leipzig. Reiter then undertook post-graduate training in bacteriology and hygiene.

The University of Leipzig

This prolonged study was exceptionally thorough and highly cosmopolitan. It was calculated to embrace training under the greatest masters in bacteriology in all Europe, and there are but few, if any, who have emulated Reiter in this respect. Commencing with nine months at the Pasteur Institute, Paris, Reiter spent a year at the Institute of Hygiene and Pharmacology at Berlin University. He then undertook two years' training under Sir Almroth Wright at St. Mary's Hospital, London. This was followed by two years as Assistant and Lecturer at the Institute of Hygiene, Königsberg. In May 1914 Reiter was elected deputy Head of a special ward at the Institute for Hygiene, Berlin. August of that year found him an assistant doctor in the German army on the

Sir Almroth Wright, 1861–1947. Professor of Bacteriology, St. Mary's Hospital, London.

Western Front, and in September, while stationed at Chauny, France, he was called upon to care for a number of soldiers suffering from Weil's disease. It was here that he made his first great discovery—he found the causative organism of Weil's disease, the *Leptospira icterohaemorrhagiae* by inoculating innumerable animals. This was a remarkable achievement, seeing that the causative organism of Weil's disease had been sought unsuccessfully since 1880. Promoted to a higher rank, Reiter was transferred to the Balkan Front. In 1916 a patient was sent to him with severe inflammation of the conjunctivae, the urethra and a number of joints. Reiter published an account of this disease in the *Deutsche medizinische Wochenschrift* in 1916; soon afterwards others reported similar cases, and it was not long before the syndrome of abacterial urethritis, conjunctivitis and arthritis became known universally as Reiter's disease.

After World War I Hans Reiter became eminent in the field of preventive medicine. He was successively Professor of Hygiene at Rostock University (1919–1923), Chief of a department of the Hygiene Institute in that city (1923–1925), Chief of a department in the Kaiser Wilhelm Institute of Experimental Therapy, Berlin, under Professor August von Wasserman, Director of the Health Department of Mecklenburg, and finally President of the Health Service in Berlin and Honorary Professor of Hygiene in the University of Berlin. From October 1933 to 1945 he represented Germany at the International Health Organisation in Paris.

One of the innovations Reiter made while occupying the Chair of Hygiene in Rostock was to make special trips with his students to various industrial centres in Germany, where he lectured on social hygiene. Professor Reiter was a Gold Medallist, University of Leipzig (1957), a Robert Koch Medallist, holder of the Grand Order of the Red Cross, and an Honorary Member of many scientific associations at home and abroad. In later years he made an intensive study of the illegitimate child and its problems.

Adolph Weil, 1848–1916. Director of the Medical Clinic, Dorpat, Esthonia. Developed laryngeal tuberculosis and subsequently practised at various spas.
August von Wassermann (see p. 233).

THE ARGYLL
ROBERTSON PUPIL

DOUGLAS
ARGYLL
ROBERTSON
1837–1909

Douglas Argyll Robertson was born in Edinburgh, the son of John Argyll Robertson, M.D. Douglas received his early education at Edinburgh and passed on to the University there; later he studied at Dundee, where he graduated M.D. St. Andrews in 1857. After a short period spent as house surgeon at the Edinburgh Royal Infirmary, he went to Berlin to study ophthalmology under Albrecht van Graefe, the leading ophthalmologist of the day.

On his return from Germany he became an assistant in the University of Edinburgh and conducted the first course of practical physiology ever held there. During this period he proved that

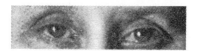

Argyll Robertson pupils. They are
small and do not react to light. The
patient has tabes dorsalis

eserine, derived from the calabar bean, led to constriction of the pupil, a discovery which has proved of great benefit to sufferers from glaucoma. In 1868, at the age of 30, he became assistant ophthalmic surgeon to the Royal Infirmary.

Douglas's father, although a general surgeon, had taken special interest in diseases of the eye and was one of the founders of the Edinburgh Eye Dispensary. It is therefore more than likely that he suggested and encouraged his son to specialise entirely in ophthal-

John Argyll Robertson, 1801–1857. Surgeon, Edinburgh Royal Infirmary.
Albrecht von Graefe, 1828–1870. Professor of Ophthalmology, Berlin. Founder of modern
* ophthalmic surgery and well known for his sign of exophthalmos.*

mology, and young Argyll Robertson was the first surgeon in
Scotland to devote himself exclusively to the practice of ophthalmic
surgery. In this speciality he achieved great eminence and one of
his discoveries, that of the 'Argyll Robertson pupil' (1869), has
perpetuated his name. He showed, by a number of clinical observations, that this peculiar phenomenon connected with the pupil
was associated with tabes dorsalis and it is today regarded as
practically conclusive evidence of syphilis of the nervous system.
The site of the lesion is probably between the oculomotor (III)
nucleus and the lateral geniculate body.

The old Royal Infirmary, Edinburgh. Foundation stone laid 1738. Opened 1741
Demolished 1879

Argyll Robertson became full ophthalmic surgeon to the Edinburgh Royal Infirmary in 1870. In 1886 he was elected President of
the Royal College of Surgeons of Edinburgh and he was the first
President (1893–95) of the Ophthalmological Society to be chosen
from amongst those practising outside London. He was surgeon
oculist in Scotland to Queen Victoria and later to King Edward
VII. As an operator he was brilliant and resourceful and he
introduced several new technical procedures. He had married in
1882, but had no family, and he and Mrs. Robertson undertook the
care and education of Prince and Princess Taraba, son and daughter
of an Indian potentate who had been one of Robertson's pupils. In
1904 Argyll Robertson retired from practice and made his home in
Jersey.

In his later years Argyll Robertson travelled widely and it was
during a third visit to India that he died at Gondal, on 3rd January,
1909. He was cremated on the banks of the River Gondhi. Argyll
Robertson was a man of splendid physique and dignified bearing,

with a fine, intellectual head. Golf he considered the finest recreation in the world and to it he attributed much of his good health. He was one of the leading amateur players of his day and five times won the gold medal of the Royal and Ancient Club, St. Andrews, Scotland.

ROENTGEN RAYS
(SYN. X-RAYS)

WILHELM
CONRAD
ROENTGEN
1845–1923

On the night of 8th November, 1895, Professor Roentgen was investigating the phenomena accompanying the passage of an electric current through a vacuum tube. The laboratory was in darkness and the tube with which he was working was covered by black cardboard, which made it impervious to any light known. To his astonishment Roentgen noticed that, when the discharge was passed through the tube, some crystals which lay upon a table some distance away became brilliantly illuminated. He placed some of the crystals at a greater distance from the tube, yet still the mysterious fluorescence could be demonstrated. He then placed materials of increasing density between the tube and the crystals. First he used a book, then wood and then plates of various metals. All proved transparent to the rays in different degrees. Finally he placed his own hand in the path of the rays and saw that the bones within it were outlined clearly. From this it was but a short step to substitute a photographic plate for the fluorescent screen—and the science of radiography was born.

Roentgen reported his discovery to the Medical Society of Würzburg, and the rays he christened X-rays.

Wilhelm Conrad Roentgen was born in the Rhineland town of Lennep. His mother was Dutch and his father German, and they were cousins and came from a family of well-known merchants. When Wilhelm was three years old the Roentgens moved to Apeldoorn, Holland, and when the boy reached school age he was sent to Utrecht, where at the age of 16 he enrolled at the technical college. From Utrecht he passed on to the University of Zürich, where he obtained the Ph.D. with a thesis on *The Study of Gases*.

About this time the lecturer on physics under whom Roentgen studied was called to the chair in the subject at Würzburg, and Roentgen, now aged 24, was appointed as his first assistant. Three years later Roentgen married a Dutch lady six years his senior, who was to be his help-mate for 50 years. When Roentgen was 34 years of age he was elected Professor of Physics at Giessen in Central Germany. In 1888 Professor Roentgen was chosen as director of the newly established physical laboratory connected with the University of Würzburg; it was here that Roentgen made his epoch-making discovery.

Roentgen was a tall, dark slender man with finely chiselled features. Incidentally, he was colour blind. He was a scientist who lived for science, and he steadfastly refused multitudinous offers to commercialise his discovery, and thereby reap rich financial rewards. Of honours he received many, among which were the Nobel Prize, the Rumford Gold Medal of the Royal Society, and the M.D. Würzburg. In 1900 he accepted the Chair of Physics at Munich, but having refused a German title that was offered to him, it would appear that he was not well received in that city.

Roentgen wrote little; the total number of his papers on X-rays number three. He died in 1923 after a long illness, and because of post-war inflation, a very poor man. Even his Nobel Prize money of 50,000 Swedish kroner he had given to the University of Würzburg to promote scientific study. His remains were laid to rest in the cemetery at Giessen, beside those of his wife, who had predeceased him.

SIMS' SPECULUM
SIMS' POSITION

JAMES
MARION
SIMS
1813–1883

In 1845 James Marion Sims, a surgeon-practitioner of Mount Meigs, Alabama, was called to attend a woman who had fallen from a horse and suffered a retroflexion of the uterus. In making a digital examination by the vaginal route with the patient on her knees, suddenly the displacement rectified itself and the patient

Sims' Speculum

was relieved of her symptoms. When she turned on to her back Sims noticed a considerable expulsion of air from the vagina. He surmised that the knee-chest position, by favouring the entry of air into the vagina, aided the replacement of the uterus.

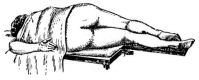

Sims' Position

207

Soon after this incident Sims devised his speculum (at first a bent spoon) to aid in the admittance of air. Subsequently he discovered that the left lateral position was as effective for vaginal examination as the knee-chest position.

Sims was born in Lancaster, South Carolina. He graduated from Jefferson Medical College, Philadelphia, in 1835, and spent 18 years in general practice in the Southern states before beginning his career as a specialist in New York.

In 1835 he operated successfully for an enormous intra-abdominal abscess (probably appendiceal in origin), containing several quarts of pus and in 1837 removed both the upper and lower jaw of a patient. This was before the days of antisepsis and anaesthesia!

The State Hospital for Women, New York

He became interested in the very troublesome condition of vesico-vaginal fistula, a condition which had so far resisted all attempts at operative treatment. There were many sufferers from this condition among the black slave population of the district in which he practised, consequent upon difficult childbirth, and in 1852 Sims published the description of an operation which revolutionised the handling of these cases and proved a boon to womankind.

Sims' technique for the repair of vesico-vaginal fistula owed its success to his use of the left lateral posture, which made visualisation easier and better, to his vaginal speculum which exposed the opening of the fistula, to the silver wire sutures he employed and to the use of a catheter for keeping the bladder empty until the fistulous tract had healed. Following the favourable reception of his paper, in 1852, at the age of 41, Sims decided to become a gynaecological specialist, and he removed to New York City.

Statue of Marion Sims in Bryant Park opposite the
New York Academy of Medicine

In 1855 he established the State Hospital for Women, which soon became a Mecca for visiting gynaecologists.

During the American Civil War, Sims, for political reasons, moved to Europe and resided in London and Paris for six years. He performed his operation for vesico-vaginal fistula before the famous surgeons, Nélaton and Velpeau, and other surgical leaders. Sims' successes where others had failed led to calls for his professional services from all over Europe.

Auguste Nélaton, 1807–1873. Surgeon, Hôpital St. Louis, Paris. Among other accomplishments he invented the rubber catheter, but it was left to:
James Archibald Jaques, 1815–1877, the Works Manager at a rubber factory in England, to perfect the patent the soft rubber catheter.
Alfred-Armand-Louis Velpeau, 1795–1867. Surgeon, the Charité. Wrote a treatise on diseases of the breast, the most important work on the subject in its time. He is known also for Velpau's bandage for the treatment of fractured clavicle.

When he at length returned to America, Sims was the best-known gynaecological surgeon in the world. Among his later contributions to gynaecological surgery were his method of amputating the cervix uteri, and an enquiry into the causes and treatment of vaginismus. In 1856 he published his *Clinical Notes on Uterine Surgery*, which was translated into German.

Sims was said to be 'a kind-hearted but impulsive man.' He died in his seventieth year.

STENSEN'S DUCT

NIELS
STENSEN
1638–1686

Niels Stensen was born at Copenhagen, the son of a court jeweller. He studied medicine in his native city and later at Leyden in the Netherlands.

One morning in April, 1661, while dissecting the head of a sheep in the house of his professor, Stensen noticed that he could pass a probe down a channel from the parotid gland. He passed the probe again and heard it click against the teeth. Stensen had discovered the duct of the parotid gland.

Soon afterwards he examined other glands, such as the lacrimal, and was able to prove that all secreting glands have ducts. This great discovery was made when Stensen was only 22 years of age. By the time he was 24, he had made other notable anatomical discoveries, which he incorporated in a book.

One of his chief interests at this time was the study of the brain, and on one of his visits to Paris (1664) he gave a celebrated discourse on cerebral anatomy and criticised the fanciful views that were held at that time.

After leaving the Netherlands he travelled widely in Germany, France and Italy. About six months after Stensen's arrival in Italy, fishermen off Leghorn landed an enormous shark. The head was transported to Florence and place at Stensen's disposal for examination. The dissection gave him an opportunity to seek the solution as to whether shark's teeth were, in fact, a component of certain fossils. From this study emerged a short treatise which is acclaimed to be the foundation of the science of palaeontology and geology.

Stensen was an accomplished linguist and had a full command of eight languages, in addition to his native Danish. It is possible that this gift of tongues was partially responsible for his restless disposition that would not allow him to settle in his homeland, or in any of the countries that he visited.

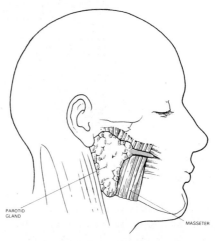

PAROTID
GLAND

MASSETER

Dissection showing Stensen's Duct

Stensen's contributions to anatomy are so amazing as to be almost unbelievable. He demonstrated Peyer's patches before Peyer; he maintained that the human ovary produced ova; he was the first to show that the mucous membrane of the nose, palate and throat secreted mucus by virtue of small glands in its deeper layers. Perhaps one of his greatest discoveries was the mechanisms of lacrimation; until Stensen's time, learned men thought that the tears were formed in the brain, and were led through the nerves to the eyes. Stensen blasted this theory by a perfect description of the whole lacrimal apparatus in 1662. At the age of 33 he published the first case of Fallot's tetralogy, a form of congenital heart disease, so-named after Louis Arthur Fallot redescribed it in 1888. Stensen's contributions to physiology are not insignificant. For instance, he showed that the muscle fibre is the contractile element, whereas previously it was considered that the tendon was the 'primary instrument of the movement.'

Johann Peyer, 1653–1712. Professor of Medicine, Schaffhausen, Switzerland.
Etienne-Louis Arthur Fallot, 1850–1911. Professor of Medicine, Marseilles.

In 1667 Stensen met a pious and learned lady, who was instrumental in converting him from Lutheranism to Roman Catholicism.

A convert of such fame was received warmly by the Church. It was not long before he applied himself to religion with that diligence and self-denial which characterised his every undertaking. In 1672 he returned to Copenhagen, but within two years we find him back again in Florence.

At the age of 36 he took holy orders. The following year he was made a bishop and was sent as Vicar Apostolic to the northern countries of Europe. Thereafter, for nine years he lived in Germany.

The University of Copenhagen in the seventeenth century. The central building is the anatomical theatre. The Church of Our Lady is seen in the background

It was not unusual for him to preach in three languages on the same day. He worked from morning to night in the service of the Church and for the welfare of the poor.

It is said that his life of self-denial undermined his health. He died at the early age of 48. By command of the Duke of Tuscany, his body was taken to Florence and buried with public honours.

Martin Luther, 1483–1546. Professor of Theology (orthodox Roman Catholic) at the University of Wittenberg until 1517, when he was excommunicated for his unorthodox views. He founded the Lutheran Church.

So passed a man possessed of one of the most agile brains of the seventeenth century.

On the wall of the San Lorenzo Church in Florence, near his tomb, is a plaque set up in the year 1888 by the world's geologists who reverence his name. Beneath it is the following inscription which commences: *Friend you behold the likeness of Nicolaus Steno. To it more than a thousand men of learning from all parts of the world contributed.*

SYME'S
AMPUTATION

JAMES
SYME
1799–1870

James Syme was born in Princes Street, Edinburgh, in 1799, the second son of an Edinburgh lawyer, or Writer to the Signet. He was educated at the High School of Edinburgh, and at the age of 16 he proceeded to Edinburgh University, becoming a pupil of Dr. Barclay. He never attended a course of lectures on surgery. While he was a student, Syme was very interested in chemistry, and he discovered that india-rubber was soluble in naphtha, and further that the rubber solution, when applied to cloth, rendered the cloth waterproof. Had Syme patented his discovery he might have made a fortune; this was done later by Charles Macintosh of Glasgow, whose name is still associated with waterproofed fabric.

In 1820, while still a final year medical student, he was appointed Superintendent of the local fever hospital. In 1821 he became a Member of the Royal College of Surgeons of England. The story of his association with his cousin, Liston, who was five years his senior, in establishing an extramural school of anatomy, and acting as Liston's assistant in private practice, has been told already (see p. 146). In 1824, after the breach between Liston and himself, Syme paid a visit to the German medical schools, and on his return he opened a private hospital, known as Minto House. This proved very successful, and in addition to treating surgical patients, Syme

John Barclay, 1758–1826. M.D. Edin., F.R.C.P. Edin. Lecturer on Anatomy and Surgery, University of Edinburgh.
Charles Macintosh, 1766–1843. F.R.S. Chemist. In addition to his work on waterproof fabrics, he made important contributions to the chemistry of dyes and to the manufacture of iron and steel.

took apprentices, and became a very popular clinical teacher—so popular, in fact, that his clinic rivalled the official school of medicine, the Edinburgh Royal Infirmary. It is therefore hardly surprising that when a vacancy occurred at the Royal Infirmary in 1829, Syme failed to obtain that envied position. The first holder of the Chair of Regius Professor of Clinical Surgery, James Russell, had never been an inspiring teacher, and by the time he had passed his eightieth year delivered lectures that contemporaries described as somnolent. At the age of 81 he offered to resign, on condition that his successor paid him £300 a year for the remainder of his life. Syme acquiesced, and having gained the Chair, the infuriated Governors were *ipso facto* compelled to allot the new Professor beds in the Royal Infirmary. A few months later, Liston left for London, and Syme succeeded to the great part of the former's private practice: thenceforth Syme's rise to fame was meteoric.

Syme's knife

Syme was a dapper little man, but his physique and small hands did not allow him to be so brilliant or rapid with the amputation knife as to emulate the *tour de maitre* of some of the pre-Listerian masters. Neither did he excel at lithotomy, at which operation a long finger was of great advantage in removing the bladder stone through a perineal incision. He was, however, a prince of clinicians, a remarkably good lecturer, a patient investigator and a careful operator, well versed in the anatomy of the regions he traversed.

Syme's name is perpetuated by his amputation. Before 1844, when Syme reported this operation, the lowest level at which surgeons would amputate was about half-way down the tibia. In suitable cases Syme amputated through the ankle joint and with the Syme's knife keeping close to the bone he cut a flap from the superficial structures of the heel. The bones were then sawn through just above the articular surface of the tibia. Syme's amputation is a good amputation for severe trauma to the foot, and many patients are able to get about without an artificial limb.

James Russell, 1754–1836. Regius Professor of Clinical Surgery, Edinburgh.
Robert Liston (see p. 145).

When Liston died in 1847, Syme was elected to fill his place at University College Hospital, London, but not liking the atmosphere, he resigned within a few months and returned to Edinburgh, and took up his former appointment, which had not been filled. It was in 1853, when James Syme, aged 54, was at the height of his fame, and accredited by many to be the first surgeon in Europe, that Joseph Lister arrived in Edinburgh and presented his credentials to Professor Syme. Syme, who was a man of strong likes and dislikes,

Syme's Amputation: it is essentially a
disarticulation at the ankle joint

took an immediate liking to Lister, and it was not long before Syme made Lister a supernumerary clerk, and later his house-surgeon. About this time Syme's private assistant died of cholera in the Crimea. This created a vacancy on the Infirmary staff, and Lister succeeded in his application for the post of Assistant Surgeon at the Edinburgh Royal Infirmary. Not long afterwards Lister married Syme's daughter.

Syme was one of the first surgeons on this side of the Atlantic to adopt ether anaesthesia, and in 1868 he was Lister's first convert to the antiseptic method.

Syme was a genial, happy man, with an intense love of flowers. His contemporaries said that he never wasted a word, a drop of ink, or a drop of blood.

Lord Lister (see p. 139).

THIERSCH
SKIN GRAFT

KARL
THIERSCH
1822–1895

Karl Thiersch was born in Munich. After studying at Berlin, Vienna and Paris, he graduated in medicine at the university of his native city.

In 1850 he took part in the war between Prussia and Denmark, serving under the great orthopaedic surgeon Stromeyer, whose teaching and example had much influence on him. After the war had finished Thiersch was appointed Professor of Surgery at the University of Erlangen, a post which he held for 13 years. In 1857 he was transferred to the Chair of Surgery at Leipzig, which he held for 28 years. During the Franco-Prussian war of 1870, he was made Consulting Surgeon to the 12th Army Corps.

With the skin stretched to the fullest
degree, the graft is cut with a razor or
special knife

George Friedrich Louis Stromeyer, 1804–1876. Professor of Surgery, Kiel, has been called the Founder of Orthopaedic Surgery, in that it was he who introduced the subcutaneous tenotomy.

Professor Thiersch, who had a considerable reputation as a practical surgeon, was an early follower of the antiseptic method of Lister.

Although Thiersch made comparatively few contributions to surgical literature, his name lives as the inventor of the Thiersch

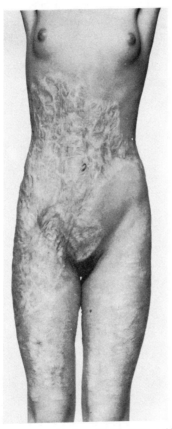

The late result of a split skin (Thiersch)
graft for an extensive burn

graft, which he described at a meeting of the German Surgical Society in 1874. A Thiersch graft comprises a thin sheet of skin, consisting of the epidermis and superficial part of the dermis, which is cut by means of a razor, a special skin graft knife or a dermatome.

Lord Lister (see p. 139).

The thigh is a particularly suitable donor area. The defect re-epithelialises from islands of epithelium left behind at the cut ends of hair follicles and sweat and sebaceous ducts. These islands coalesce and the area heals completely within two or three weeks. Indeed, it can be harvested again if necessary for further grafting. The Thiersch graft itself, placed on a raw defect such as a granulating wound, receives its nourishment first from diffusion of tissue fluid then, after three of four days, by the ingrowth of capillaries from the wound bed.

Carl Thiersch died at Leipzig at the age of 73.

THOMAS'S SPLINT
THOMAS'S WRENCH

HUGH
OWEN
THOMAS
1834–1891

The story of Hugh Owen Thomas in one of the most amazing in the history of medicine. The son of a bone-setter, the whole of his professional life was spent in general practice in the slums of Liverpool, yet he did more than anyone before him to advance the treatment of diseases of bones and joints.

Thomas came from a family of bone-setters of Anglesey, whose secrets had been handed down from father to son for many generations. His father, Evan Thomas, had migrated to Liverpool at the age of 19, and had acquired a great reputation there by the practice of his art. He was determined that his son should receive the benefits of a regular medical education, and Hugh was apprenticed for four years to his uncle, Dr. Owen Roberts of St. Asaph, North Wales. Later he studied at Edinburgh and at University College, London, qualifying M.R.C.S. in 1857.

After spending a few weeks in Paris, where he much admired the skill of the French surgical instrument makers, Thomas returned to Liverpool to help his father. He found, however, that the rule of thumb methods of the bone-setter were uncongenial, and in 1859 moved to a different part of the city, and set up practice independently.

He soon gained a great reputation, at first among the poor people, and then among the better classes in Liverpool and its environs. He held a clinic every Sunday morning, at which he treated poor people gratuitously.

The cardinal theme in Thomas's creed was the necessity for **Rest** 'enforced, uninterrupted and prolonged,' and he carried this principle into effect in all his treatments. Immobilisation in the

221

treatment of fractures has been practised since the earliest times, but in Thomas's day excision and amputation were almost the routine methods adopted for chronic diseases of joints. Thomas applied the principle of complete rest in these cases also, and did much to revolutionise the treatment of tuberculous joints. He insisted that while rest was the first requisite it must be applied in such a way that the diseased part was neither compressed, nor the normal circulation of the limb impaired. With this end in view, Thomas invented most of the fracture splints now in use. These

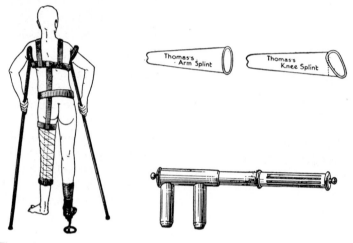

Thomas's Hip Splint in use   Thomas's Wrench

splints were made in his own workshop and he kept a blacksmith and a saddler employed constantly. Thomas also invented a wrench for the reduction of fractures, and an osteoclast to break deformed bones before resetting them. The secret of his success was his mechanical genius and attention to detail. The outstanding feature of his apparatus was its extreme simplicity. The work of Thomas would never have attained recognition had it not been for his nephew and pupil, Sir Robert Jones, and the opportunities provided by the First World War. Thanks to the more general use of the Thomas splint, the mortality of compound fracture of the femur fell from 80 per cent in 1916 to 7·3 per cent in 1918.

Sir Robert Jones, 1858–1933. Surgeon, Royal Southern Hospital, Liverpool.

Hugh Owen Thomas's house at 11, Nelson Street, Liverpool

Thomas was a thin, dark, fragile little man. He had an accident while a student which resulted in a deformed eyelid, and rather spoiled the expression of his face. He had indomitable energy, and worked from six in the morning until midnight, never taking a holiday. He was always dressed in a black frock coat buttoned up at the neck, with a peaked naval cap tilted over his defective eyelid. He smoked cigarettes almost continuously, and was seldom seen without one in his mouth.

During his lifetime, Thomas's work did not receive the recognition which was his due; today he is acknowledged as a great pioneer in orthopaedic surgery, and a great benefactor of mankind.

TRENDELENBURG'S POSITION

FRIEDRICH TRENDELENBURG
1844–1924

Trendelenburg's position is used for many gynaecological and other intra-pelvic operations. Its inestimable value is that the intestines can be packed away from the field of operation, leaving the pelvis free from coils. The position was first described with the permission of his 'venerable chief' by Willy Meyer, who had been a student under Professor Trendelenburg at Bonn in 1881.

Trendelenburg's position

Friedrich Trendelenburg was born in Berlin. He had the unusual experience of pursuing his early medical studies in Glasgow, and returning to Germany to complete his training he graduated M.D. Berlin in 1866. From 1868 to 1874 he was assistant to Professor Langenbeck, after which he was appointed surgeon to the Friedrichshain Hospital, Berlin. A few years later he was called to the

H. Willy Meyer, 1858–1952. Surgeon, Lennox Hill Hospital, New York.
Berhard von Langenbeck, 1810–1887. Professor of Surgery, Berlin.

Chair of Surgery at Rostock, from thence to Bonn, and finally to Leipzig.

Trendelenburg took a leading part in the great advance of surgery during the latter part of the nineteenth century. He founded the German Society of Surgeons, and was its president and historian. Professor Trendelenburg wrote much, and did exceptional work in the fields of plastic surgery, congenital dislocation of the hip-joint and the surgery of blood-vessels, besides making an international

The Surgical Institute, Leipzig, where Trendelenburg worked

reputation as a gynaecological surgeon. Trendelenburg's name is associated with two clinical tests, one for confirming shortening of a leg due to an ununited fracture of the neck of the femur or congenital dislocation of the hip-joint and the other for detecting incompetence of the valves of the veins of the thigh. As stated on page 26, the latter test, known universally as Trendelenburg's test, was described by Sir Benjamin Brodie many years before it was published by Trendelenburg.

When he was 64 years of age, Trendelenburg devised and carried out an operation for removal of the blood-clot blocking the pulmonary artery in pulmonary embolism, but he never met with success. On his 80th birthday one of his pupils, Kirschner,

Sir Benjamin Brodie (see p. 25).
Martin Kirschner, 1879–1942. Professor of Surgery, University of Heidelberg, Germany.

demonstrated a patient upon whom he (Kirschner) had performed successfully pulmonary embolectomy.

This great practical surgeon was keenly interested in the history of surgery, and wrote a valuable work on ancient Indian surgery and a fascinating autobiography. The closing years of his life were spent at Nikolassee, Germany. He died in his 81st year as a result of carcinoma of the lower jaw.

VINCENT'S ANGINA (STOMATITIS)

HYACINTHE VINCENT 1862–1950

Hyacinthe Vincent established beyond reasonable doubt that exceptionally a pyogenic affection is due to symbiotic infection. This means that the infection is due to two organisms living in harmony, and, having joined partnership, neither is able to effect destruction of human tissue without the other. The dual infection Vincent discovered, now known as Vincent's angina (or stomatitis or infection), is due to the *Fusobacterium plauti-vincenti* and a spirochaete subsequently called the *Borrelia vincenti*.

Borrelia vincenti and *F. plauti-vincenti*

Born in Bordeaux, after a brilliant school career Hyacinthe Vincent studied medicine, at first in his native city, and then in Paris, where in 1887 he graduated M.D., winning the prize for the best thesis. Against the advice of his professors, who recommended this brilliant student to pursue an academic career, Vincent chose the Army Medical Service, and in 1888 he presented himself for the examination for entry to the famous military medical college, Val-de-Grâce. Once more he gained first place. On completing the usual course of military training, he was commissioned Médecin Aide-Major, second class, and was assigned to the bacteriological laboratory of the college. In 1891 Major Vincent was posted to the military hospital at Algiers, where he served for five years, and where he established the first army bacteriological laboratory.

The Val-de-Grâce Military Hospital and School, Rue Saint-Jacques, Paris V^e

In 1894 Vincent discovered the organism responsible for Madura foot, the *Oöspora madurae*. In 1896 he made the discovery that perpetuates his name in the following way: Forty-seven wounded African soldiers were admitted to the hospital in Algiers. From their suppurating wounds Vincent isolated the symbiotic organisms referred to above. In later years he extended this study, and found these organisms were the cause of the ulcero-membranous stomatitis, known during the 1914–18 war as 'trench mouth.' Towards the end of 1896 Vincent was transferred to Marseilles where, as in Algiers, he established a bacteriological laboratory. A year later, at the age of 35, he was nominated Professor agrégé in Forensic Medicine at Val-de-Grâce. In 1901 Vincent was called to the Chair of Bacteriology and Epidemiology at Val-de-Grâce, and it was here that he founded a laboratory for the making of anti-typhoid vaccine. This vaccine was tried among the troops in North Africa, and was found to be effective.

During the first winter of World War I typhoid raged among the French troops in the trenches, and there was a mortality of more than 25 per cent. Vincent sought an interview with the President of the Council of Ministers, and convinced him of the imperative necessity for vigorous action. The next day Vincent was given special powers, and, proceeding to the Western Front, he supervised the anti-typhoid vaccination of the troops. Not long afterwards Marshal Foch said of Vincent that he had won 'a medical battle of the Marne.'

Vincent was promoted Médecin Général in 1917, and on him were bestowed the most prized honours in the gift of the French Republic; among others he was awarded the Grand Croix de la Légion d'Honneur. In 1950, when he was on his death-bed, he was invested with the Médaille Militaire. This honour, which is hardly if ever given except to combatant soldiers, was especially voted by the Council of Ministers in recognition of his services to the army and to humanity.

The attainment of the highest rung often prevents the holder from pursuing research, but not so Vincent. The list of his advancements of medical knowledge is formidable. It includes cerebro-spinal fever, Malta fever, cholera, tetanus and meningitis.

In 1924 he was retired from the army under the age limit, but in the following year he was appointed Professor of the Collège de France, the chair being created especially for him. At the same time he continued to work in a small laboratory at Val-de-Grâce, and published papers on varying subjects until shortly before his death, which occurred at the age of 87 years. So passed the greatest bacteriologist the army of France had ever known.

Marshal Ferdinand Foch, O.M., 1851–1929. Chief of the Allied Armies in France, 1917–1918.

VOLKMANN'S ISCHAEMIC CONTRACTURE

VOLKMANN'S MEMBRANE

VOLKMANN'S SPOON

RICHARD
VON VOLKMANN
1830–1889

The whole of Richard von Volkmann's professional life was spent at Halle, in Saxony, where his father had held the chair of anatomy and physiology. Richard studied at several universities and graduated M.D. Berlin at the age of 24. Two years later he was appointed

The University Clinic, Halle, in the time of Richard von Volkmann

to act as deputy professor of the Surgical Clinic at Halle, and in 1867 he became the professor. When Volkmann took over from his predecessor, hospital gangrene was so rife in Halle that it was said that 'no one dared to touch a knife in the surgical clinic.'

On assuming full control of the clinic, Volkmann, who had

230

studied everything that Lister had written, established *in toto* the antiseptic method in his hospital. He became Lister's most powerful advocate in Germany. Sir George Makins, who visited Volkmann's clinic at Halle in 1879, has left a vivid description of Volkmann's methods. The most striking feature of his operating theatre was the terazza paving, so arranged as to allow efficient drainage. This was a very important matter because, in addition to the Lister spray, irrigating the wounds freely with 1 in 20 carbolic lotion was always employed during operations. The surgeons and assistants all wore long rubber boots, and as soon as Volkmann called 'watering can,' this lotion was poured out with great freedom from gardeners' watering cans with long spouts. The slogan of the clinic was 'If dirt be unavoidable, it must be antiseptic dirt.'

Volkmann made many contributions to surgery, and was an elegant, bold and original operator; surgeons from all over the Continent flocked to his clinic. It was he who first drew attention

Collar-stud abscess of the neck

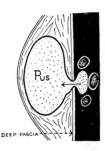

to the fact that carcinoma of the skin can result from constant exposure to irritating substances, and to this end he published an important study of cancer in paraffin workers. It was Volkmann who described the peculiar velvety, very dark red granulation tissue that lines a tuberculous abscess, particularly the superficial loculus of a collar-stud abscess of the neck. This granulation tissue, known as Volkmann's membrane, is so luxuriant that it hides the tiny opening in the deep cervical fascia through which the tuberculous pus escapes from the infected breaking-down lymph-nodes lying beneath the deep fascia. For removing this and other types of exuberant granulation tissue, e.g. that occurring in connection with

Lord Lister, 1827–1912. Professor of Surgery successively at Glasgow, Edinburgh and London.
Sir George Makins, 1853–1933. Surgeon, St. Thomas's Hospital, London.

necrosis of bone, Volkmann designed his spoon, which is still in daily use.

However, Volkmann's name is perpetuated by his ischaemic contraction (which goes by no other name) more than by any other of his contributions to knowledge.

He first described ischaemic contracture in 1872, subsequently reporting further cases. Usually ischaemic contracture occurs in the bellies of the flexor muscles of the forearm, but it is seen occasionally

Volkmann's spoon

in a leg. It is a rapidly progressive destruction and contracture of the muscles concerned. Until 1872 this phenomenon was considered to be due to nerve injury; Volkmann showed that it was due to death of muscle fibres, the result of the arterial supply being jeopardised by too tight splinting. He demonstrated that the involved muscles underwent necrosis, their subsequent replacement by fibrous scar tissue producing the typical contracture. While the

Volkmann's ischaemic contracture

condition almost always follows a fracture, Volkmann insisted that it could result from injury to soft parts alone—a contention that has now been fully substantiated. Many cases have resulted from a too-tight plaster cast, and many legal actions for malpractice have been fought on account of the development of this contracture.

Volkmann was a striking personality, of medium height, fairly stout build, and with long Dundreary whiskers. A man of intellect and culture, he wrote delightful poems under the pen-name of 'Richard Leander.' His *Dreams by French Firesides*, containing fairy-tales written while on service during the Franco-Prussian war, made a great impression in Germany and passed through no fewer than 14 editions.

He died at Jena at the comparatively early age of 59 years.

THE WASSERMANN REACTION

AUGUST VON WASSERMANN
1866–1925

The names of many members of the medical profession have been perpetuated because they have discovered a disease, sign or test. In the case of August von Wassermann not only has his name become part of the medical vocabulary of all countries, but the term 'Wassermann Reaction' has been abbreviated to the first letters of each word, viz. W.R., and these letters alone remind us of his great achievement. No sign in what may be termed 'medical shorthand' is so well-known or carries such ominous significance as 'W.R.+.'

The Wassermann Reaction for the sero-diagnosis of syphilis was discovered by Wassermann and his associates, Neisser and Brück, in 1906. It followed almost immediately upon two discoveries of fundamental importance: the demonstration by Metchnikoff and Roux in 1903 that syphilis could be inoculated in apes, and the discovery in 1905 by Schaudinn and Hoffmann of the organism of the disease, the *Treponema pallidum*.

Wassermann's discovery was based on a mass of work by earlier bacteriologists, and especially on the researches of the Belgians, Bordet and Gengou, into the phenomenon of 'complement fixation.'

Albert Ludwig Siegmund Neisser, 1855–1916. Professor of Skin and Venereal Diseases, Breslau. He recognised the gonococcus in 1879.
Carl Brück, 1879–1944. Physician, University Clinic for Skin Diseases, Breslau.
Elie Metchnikoff, 1845–1916. Professor of Biology, Odessa. Later became Sub-director of the Pasteur Institute, Paris.
Émile Roux, 1853–1933. Director of the Pasteur Institute, Paris.
Fritz Schaudinn, 1871–1906. Director of Protozoölogy, The Kaiser Wilhelm Institute, Berlin.
Jules Bordet, 1870–1961. Honorary Professor, University of Brussels. Formerly Director of the Pasteur Institute, Brussels.
Erich Hoffmann, 1868–1959. Professor and Director, University Polyclinic for Skin Diseases, Bonn, from 1910 to 1934.
Octave Gengou, 1875–1957. Bacteriologist, Institute of Hygiene, University of Brussels.

233

Stated in its simplest form, the principle of complement fixation depends on the fact that foreign organic substances, such as pathogenic bacteria, stimulate the formation in the blood of antibodies designed to destroy the invading organisms. Bordet and Gengou devised tests for the detection of these antibodies in the blood serum, and Wassermann succeeded in applying similar methods to the detection of antibodies in the serum of syphilitic monkeys. The test was soon developed as a practical one for the diagnosis of syphilis in man, and it also proved to be of great value in estimating the activity of the disease process.

The Kaiser Wilhelm Institute,
Berlin

The mechanism of the Wassermann reaction depends on the detection of a cross-reacting antibody to Cardiolipin in beef heart muscle. The test itself is over-sensitive, with a proportion of false positive reactions. It has now been replaced by tests which nevertheless retain the underlying principle of the original W.R. test, particularly the demonstration of Fluorescent Treponemal Antibody (F.T.A.).

August von Wassermann was born in Bamberg, Bavaria. He was pupil of Robert Koch and was associated with the Koch Institute for Infectious Diseases throughout his career. In 1907 he was placed

Robert Koch (see p. 119).

in charge of the Department of Therapeutics and Serum Research of the University of Berlin, and in 1913 became Director of the Kaiser Wilhelm Institute for Experimental Therapeutics. Early in his career Wassermann studied the antitoxin treatment of diphtheria, and he also did important work in connection with inoculation against typhoid, cholera and tetanus. His later years were occupied with research on tuberculosis and on the possibilities of sero-diagnosis in cancer.

August von Wassermann died in Berlin at the age of 59 years.

Cl. WELCHII

WILLIAM
HENRY
WELCH
1850–1934

Clóstridium welchii (or *perfringens*) is the organism most commonly associated with gas gangrene. It is an anaerobic, capsulated, spore-forming, gas-producing and gram-positive organism. Dr. Welch discovered and described the bacillus in 1892, when he was Professor of Pathology at the Johns Hopkins University, Baltimore.

William Welch, who came from a long line of members of the medical profession (his father, grandfather and great-grandfather

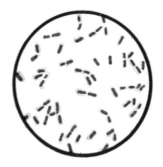

Cl. welchii

were all doctors), was born at Norfolk, Connecticut. After attending Yale University, New Haven, Connecticut, in 1872 Welch enrolled at the College of Physicians and Surgeons, New York, and there graduated in 1875. Soon after qualifying he proceeded to Europe to study under men who were creating the new science of bacteriology. The '70s and '80s of the last century were a golden age in medical discovery; few men can have had such opportunities as were given to this eager young American who went everywhere and saw everybody whose name loomed large in the vernal firmament of bacteriology.

On his return to New York in 1879 he was made Professor of Pathology at Bellevue Medical College, and held his chair until 1884, when he was appointed the first Professor of Pathology at the university which had just been founded under the will of the Baltimore millionaire, Johns Hopkins.

Professor Welch himself did notable work as a pathologist and bacteriologist, and his literary output of more than 300 papers covered an amazing range of subjects.

Professor Welch had always taken a leading part in preventive

The Johns Hopkins University, Baltimore, 1899.

medicine, and in 1916 he resigned the chair of pathology at Johns Hopkins University to become Director of the School of Hygiene and Public Health at Baltimore. At the age of 76 this remarkable man accepted a newly created post of Professor of the History of Medicine in the Johns Hopkins University, and at once set out to travel over Europe in order to purchase old medical books. In 1930 the fine library which he had created was dedicated and named in his honour the William H. Welch Medical Library.

Professor Welch was a short, thick-set little figure with twinkling blue eyes, a white moustache, and Vandyke beard. A humble, genial little man, he remained a bachelor.

Professor Welch died in Baltimore at the age of 84. He was respected as a scientist, admired as an organiser for the betterment of public health, and beloved as a teacher.

SPENCER WELLS' FORCEPS

SIR THOMAS SPENCER WELLS
1818–1897

Thomas Spencer Wells was born at St. Albans, the eldest son of William Wells, a builder. He was apprenticed to Michael Sadler, a general practitioner of Barnsley, in Yorkshire, and later he attended the General Infirmary at Leeds.

Next he studied at Trinity College, Dublin, and he completed his undergraduate training at St. Thomas's Hospital, London, before qualifying M.R.C.S. (Eng.) in 1841. He forthwith joined the Navy

The original Spencer Wells' Forceps (from the
British Medical Journal, 10th January, 1874). The
instrument was made by Krohne & Sessman

and served for six years in the Naval Hospital at Malta, where he was allowed to engage in civil practice in addition to his Naval duties. Such good reports were received concerning his work at Malta that in 1844 he was awarded the F.R.C.S. by election. His term of office at Malta being completed, he left the Navy, and soon

238

afterwards settled in Brook Street, London, as an ophthalmologist. Spencer Wells had had a large experience in obstetrics, and when a vacancy occurred in 1854 he applied and was elected Surgeon to the Samaritan Hospital. At this time the hospital consisted of only one house. On the outbreak of the Crimean war, he volunteered, and was sent first to Smyrna and afterwards to the Dardanelles, and gained great experience in gun-shot wounds. He returned to London in 1856, determined to apply the knowledge he had gained in abdominal wounds to the disease peculiar to women. At that time oöphorectomy was associated with an appalling mortality, but

Modern Spencer Wells' Forceps
ready for use

in spite of initial failures, he rose above the almost overwhelming prejudices that surrounded the performance of this operation. In 1858 he performed his first successful oöphorectomy. In 1880 he published an account of his first 1,000 cases with a mortality of 23·1 per cent. All his cases were carefully documented—failures as well as successes. By his careful methods and perseverance he was able to turn the operation into one of comparative safety.

Spencer Wells' name is perpetuated by his invention of the haemostatic forceps which bear his name. Before the invention of artery forceps, the fingers of an assistant were used to control bleeding during an operation. Wells' forceps were based upon the old artery forceps of Liston, and the crude 'bull-dogs' of the famous German surgeon, Dieffenbach. It will be seen from the illustration that the original pattern had only one catch. This idea has been improved upon, and the modern instrument has three or four.

Spencer Wells' operations were models of surgical procedure and his operating theatre at the Samaritan Hospital was thronged by surgeons from far and near. He worked in absolute silence, and submitted his assistants to a rigid discipline.

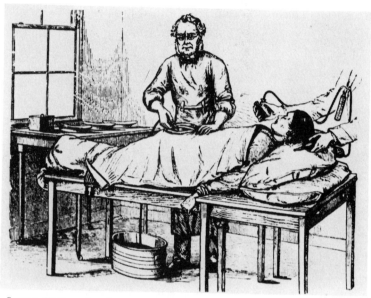

Spencer Wells performing an oöphorectomy; note the Spartan simplicity of the equipment

In 1883 Spencer Wells reached the peak of his career when he was elected President of the Royal College of Surgeons, and received a baronetcy.

In person Sir Spencer Wells was rather more than medium height, slightly portly, genial, modest, dignified and unassuming in manner. In debate his utterances were clear, positive, comprehensive but

Robert Liston (see p. 145).

Johann Friedrich Dieffenbach, 1792–1847. Surgeon to the Charité, Berlin, and later Professor at the University. Was the first to treat strabismus successfully by severing the tendons of the eye muscles.

Spencer Wells' private residence, Golders Hill Park, Golders Green

not aggressive, unless he was roused to self-defence by personal attacks upon himself or his professional career. A keen lover and a fine judge of horses, he drove himself daily in a phaeton and pair from his private residence (now Golders Hill Park) in Golders Green to his rooms in Upper Grosvenor Street. He died near Cannes in 1897 and his body was cremated at Woking.

WHARTON'S DUCT

THOMAS WHARTON
1614–1673

Thomas Wharton was an eminent physician who flourished at the time of the Restoration. He is remembered today for his description of the duct of the submandibular salivary gland—Wharton's Duct. True, this duct had been seen more than a century before by an Italian anatomist, but Wharton was the first to publish a description of it.

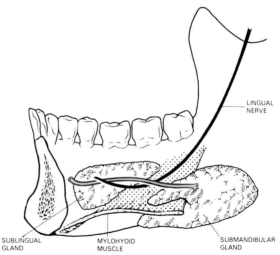

Dissection to show Wharton's Duct and the structures in relation to it (medial view).

242

Thomas Wharton was born at Winston-on-Tees. He attended the universities of both Oxford and Cambridge, and acted for some time as tutor to the illegitimate son of the Earl of Sutherland.

On the outbreak of war he removed to London and studied medicine under John Bathurst. He obtained the degree of M.D. of Oxford and also that of Cambridge.

The Plague of London. Contemporary print 1665. (Pepysian collection, Magdalene College, Cambridge.)

Dr. Wharton was one of the very few physicians who remained in London during the whole of the outbreak of the Great Plague in 1665. He was physician to St. Thomas's Hospital, and King Charles II promised to appoint him his Physician in Ordinary as soon as a vacancy should occur, on condition that he attended the Guards, who as fast as they fell ill were sent to St. Thomas's Hospital. Soon after the Plague had abated a vacancy did occur, but Charles, with the characteristic fickleness of his nature, gave the post to another.

John Bathurst, 1607–1659, M.D. Camb. and Oxford, F.R.C.P. Physician to Oliver Cromwell.
Samuel Pepys, 1633–1703. F.R.S. Civil Administrator of Royal Navy. The Diary was written while he was a comparatively young man. It includes eye witness descriptions of the Great Plague and Fire of London.

Wharton as compensation was granted a coat of arms, for which, incidentally, he had to pay £10.

Wharton was a great friend of Dr. Francis Glisson, of Glisson's capsule of the liver fame. He also had the honour of being referred to by Izaak Walton in that classic, *The Compleat Angler*. Walton thanks the doctor for help in the historical section of his work and calls him 'a dear friend that loves both me and my art of angling.'

Dr. Wharton died in harness at his house in Aldersgate Street and was buried in the church of St. Michael Bassishaw in Basinghall Street.

Francis Glisson, 1597–1677. Sometime Professor of Medicine at Cambridge, later removed to London and like Wharton, was one of the small band of physicians who continued to work there during the Great Plague.

Izaak Walton, 1593–1683. Author of The Compleat Angler, or the Contemplative Man's Recreation.

THE WIDAL TEST

FERNAND WIDAL
1862–1929

Widal's name is known throughout the world because of the serological test for typhoid fever which he described in 1896.

This confirmatory test is invaluable in the diagnosis of enteric fever, which is caused by organisms of the *Salmonella* group. It is founded on the agglutinating action of the patient's serum on these organisms. A drop of a killed suspension of any member of the group is added to a few drips of the patient's diluted blood serum. The test has evolved considerably since introduced by Widal. In present-day practice at least six suspensions are used. When the test is positive, these members of the *Salmonella* group that are responsible for the infection are seen under the microscope to be grouped together in small masses or clumps. The value of the test lies in its simplicity and the rapidity with which it can be performed. Thus infection with typhoid, paratyphoid (A) and (B), may be diagnosed with scientific accuracy.

Gruber and Durham had demonstrated that agglutination resulted from the reaction between bacteria and the serum of animals immunised against them. Widal reversed this procedure, noting that a patient's serum could be tested with bacteria of a known type, and in this way the infection from which he was suffering could be identified in the same manner. Thus Widal

Max Gruber, 1853–1927. Successively Professor of Hygiene at Graz, Vienna and Munich.
Herbert Edward Durham, 1860–1945. A pupil of Max Gruber. Research bacteriologist in tropical diseases. He served on the Royal Society's tsetse fly commission in Africa and headed the yellow fever expedition to Brazil. He accompanied the beriberi expedition to Malaya and Christmas Island. Having lost the sight of one eye in this expedition, he accepted the post of Superintendent of the Chemical Department of H. P. Bulmer and Co., cider manufacturers at Hereford.

discovered the confirmatory test for typhoid and infection by organisms of the typhoid group.

Georges Fernand Isidore Widal was born at Dellys in Algiers on 9th March, 1862. He received his medical education in Paris, and by his attainments and his application to work made his mark early in life. He took his M.D. in 1889, and when he was 27 years of age he published a treatise on *Puerperal Infection*. Laboratory work appealed to him. By 1895 he had climbed the hard road leading to a professorship in the Paris Faculty of Medicine. At first he was Professor of Internal Pathology, and later Professor of Clinical Medicine. In 1896 he obtained world-wide fame by the publication of his diagnostic test for typhoid.

Hôpital Cochin

Widal's reputation does not rest upon this work alone. He made other important discoveries in bacteriology, and was a pioneer of anti-typhoid vaccination. In 1907 he segregated acquired haemolytic anaemia from the other anaemias. All his work was characterised by experimental accuracy, and his writings are noted for their clarity and precision.

Apart from his reputation for research, Widal became widely known as a leading Paris physician, and his clinics at the Hôpital Cochin were thronged with pupils.

Professor Widal received many honours. He died from cerebral haemorrhage and was buried in the cemetery of Montmartre.

THE CIRCLE
OF WILLIS

THOMAS
WILLIS
1621–1675

Thomas Willis was born on 27th January, 1621, at Great Bedwin, in Wiltshire, the son of a farmer. He entered Christ Church, Oxford, in 1636, taking the degrees of B.A. in 1639 and M.A. in 1642.

The outbreak of the Civil War found him still resident in the city of Oxford, a Royalist stronghold, and although he bore arms for the King, he contrived to finish his medical studies. In 1646 he obtained the degree of M.B. He took his M.D. in 1660 and was made an Honorary Fellow of the Royal College of Physicians in 1664.

At Oxford Willis was a member of a group of learned men who formed themselves into a 'Philosophicall Clubbe' for the discussion of questions of science. This club was the forerunner of the Royal Society, established in 1662, of which Willis became one of the foundation Fellows.

In 1646 Willis commenced medical practice at Oxford. At this time the city had fallen into the hands of Cromwell. By the Restoration, Willis's loyalty to the Royalist cause was rewarded by the Professorship of Natural Philosophy at Oxford. In 1666 Dr. Willis left Oxford and took a house in St. Martin's Lane, London. The reputation he had acquired in Oxford stood him in good stead, and before a few years had passed no contemporary physician in the whole country had a larger practice; indeed, 'never any physician before went beyond him or got more money.'

Willis was a man of great industry. Despite his enormous

Oliver Cromwell, 1599–1658. Lord Protector of England from 1653 to his death.

practice, he found time to write a number of books and to make many original observations. His greatest and most enduring work is his *Cerebri Anatome*, which appeared in 1664. It was based upon his own dissections and gave the most complete and accurate account of the nervous system which had appeared to that date.

In this book he described the network of arteries at the base of the brain, now known as the Circle of Willis, classified the cranial

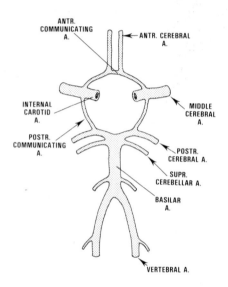

The Circle of Willis

nerves and first described the eleventh cranial nerve (the spinal accessory). A number of the illustrations to the book were drawn by that many-sided genius, Sir Christopher Wren, who had been a pupil of Willis.

Willis was the first in Europe to draw attention to the sweet taste of diabetic urine.

Willis's writings, although extremely verbose, are valuable because of the careful clinical observations which they contain. He was the first to describe and name puerperal fever, and gave excellent accounts of general paralysis and whooping-cough. Specialists in many departments of medicine have paid tribute to

Sir Christopher Wren, 1632–1723. The most famous architect England has produced. St. Paul's Cathedral is his best-known edifice.

the wide range of his observations and have drawn attention to the wonderful anticipations of modern knowledge contained in his books.

Thomas Willis died on 11th November, 1675, after a life brimful of achievement. He was buried in Westminster Abbey.

A yearly festival in honour of Willis is held on St. Martin's day at St. Martin's Church, Fenny Stratford, Bucks. There is a sermon, a dinner at the local inn and the firing of six mug-like cannonades, known as 'Fenny Poppers', by the vicar and local dignitaries. This church was built in 1731 by Browne Willis, the physician's grandson. It was dedicated to St. Martin because Thomas Willis had lived in St. Martin's Lane, London, had died on St. Martin's day (14th November) and had acquired his fame and wealth as a practitioner in the Royal Parish of St. Martin's-in-the-Fields.

WILMS'S
TUMOUR OF THE
KIDNEY

MAX
WILMS
1867–1918

Max Wilms was born near Aachen, the son of a lawyer. He studied medicine at several German universities, including Berlin, and graduated M.D. at Bonn in 1890. For some years he was assistant at the Pathological Insititute at Cologne, and it was here that he carried out research on the nature of mixed tumours, especially of the ovary.

Having gained a thorough grounding in pathology, he went to the famous Leipzig surgical clinic as an assistant to Professor

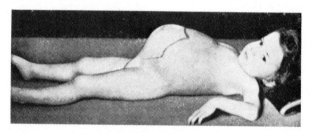

Wilms's Tumour

Trendelenburg. He continued his work on the pathology of mixed tumours (i.e. those containing a variety of different types of cells), and in 1899 published a book which cleared up much of the existing confusion about this class of neoplasm. The mixed tumour of the kidney (nephroblastoma) was thenceforth called Wilms's tumour.

Friedrich Trendelenburg (see p. 224).

This is an extremely anaplastic tumour, usually unilateral, which commonly makes its appearance during the first four years of life. Occasionally it affects older children and adolescents. It probably originates from embryonic mesodermal tissue. Under the micro-

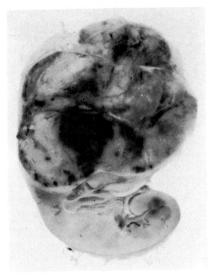

Wilms's tumour removed from a child aged four

scope there is a mixed appearance of spindle cells, epithelial tubules and smooth or striated muscle fibres. The regional lymph nodes are soon invaded and spread occurs by the blood stream to the lungs and liver.

The tumour grows rapidly to produce a large mass in the loin. Although once the prognosis was nearly always hopeless, today with nephrectomy followed by radiotherapy and cytotoxic therapy long term cures may be obtained.

Advancing in Professor Trendelenburg's Clinic, Wilms became successively teacher of surgery and, in 1904, extraordinary profes- sor. Unlike appointments in the British school of medicine, in Germany and many other countries professors move from one university to another. While this system has its disadvantages, it certainly enables a university to choose the best man from a number of candidates. Thus it was that in 1907 Max Wilms became

The University of Heidelberg

Professor of Surgery at Basle, but in 1910 he removed to Heidelberg, where he held the Chair of Surgery until his death in 1918.

Professor Wilms was a well-known surgical author. He edited a famous *Textbook of Surgery*, which was translated into five languages, but it is the work done in his youth on the pathology of mixed tumours that perpetuates his name today.

THE FORAMEN OF WINSLOW

JACOB BENIGNUS WINSLOW 1669–1760

Jacob Benignus Winslow can justly be called the creator of descriptive anatomy. His *Anatomical Exposition of the Human Body*, written in French in 1732 and translated into English two years later, was the best treatise on anatomy between the works of Vesalius (1543) and Bichat (1801). Winslow set out to collect and confirm anatomical facts and to arrange them systematically. This he did in masterly fashion.

Winslow was born at Odense, Denmark, on 2nd April, 1669, the eldest of 13 children. Most of the members of his family had followed ecclesiastical careers. Jacob's father and grandfather were both Lutheran ministers, and it was assumed that the boy would also enter the ministry. With this end in view he went through a severe course of instruction under his father, who was a very learned man, and then entered the theological faculty of the University of Copenhagen.

Winslow's great-uncle was Niels Stensen (see p. 211). The example of this illustrious relative probably induced Winslow to turn from the study of theology to that of medicine.

Winslow's achievements were recognised by the King of Denmark, who granted him a pension in order 'that the country might not be without participation in the glory of advancing the progress

Andreas Vesalius, 1514–1564. Professor of Anatomy successively in Padua, Bologna and Pisa. Marie Francois Zavier Bichat, 1771–1802. Was appointed Physician to the Hôtel Dieu in 1801, just before his premature death. Previously he was lecturer in anatomy.

of anatomical knowledge.' With the aid of this travelling fellowship he studed in Holland, and then proceeded to Paris. Here he became a student of the French anatomist, Duverney.

He graduated M.D. Paris in 1705, and continued his association with his master. So great was Winslow's ability that he deputised for Duverney in lecturing on anatomy and surgery at the Jardin du Roi. In 1743 Winslow was appointed to the chair of Physick, Anatomy and Surgery in the University of Paris, and he filled this highly important post with dignity and great distinction for 17 years.

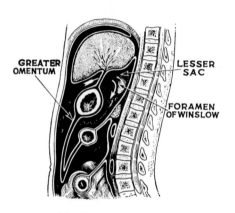

The Foramen of Winslow

In his famous book, *Exposition Anatomique de la Structure du Corps Humain*, of 1732 he described the opening which connects the two sacs of the peritoneum, known as the Foramen of Winslow. He demonstrated the communications of the foramen by inserting a quill into this opening, and then blowing air through the quill. He found that the air distended the greater omentum. Winslow is credited with having been the first to use the term omentum in its present sense.

His name is also connected with the posterior ligament of the knee joint (Winslow's ligament) and with the whorls of capillary vessels in the choroid coat of the eye (Winslow's stars). In 1732 he described the nerve ganglia as 'subordinated secondary brainlets.'

Some years after his migration to France, Winslow renounced

Joseph Guichard Duverney, 1648–1730. Professor of Anatomy, Jardin du Roi, Paris.

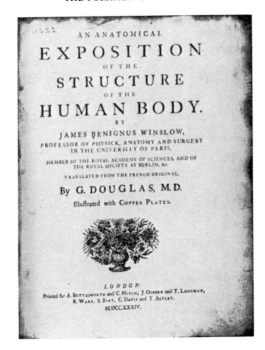

AN ANATOMICAL
EXPOSITION
OF THE
STRUCTURE
OF THE
HUMAN BODY.
BY
JAMES BENIGNUS WINSLOW,
PROFESSOR OF PHYSICK, ANATOMY AND SURGERY
IN THE UNIVERSITY OF PARIS,
MEMBER OF THE ROYAL ACADEMY OF SCIENCES, AND OF
THE ROYAL SOCIETY AT BERLIN, &c
TRANSLATED FROM THE FRENCH ORIGINAL
By G. DOUGLAS, M.D.
Illuftrated with Copper Plates.

LONDON:
Printed for A. Bettesworth and C. Hitch, J. Osborn and T. Longman,
R. Ware, S. Birt, C. Davis and T. Astley.
M.DCC.XXXIV.

the Lutheran faith, the faith of his forebears for generations, and
became a Roman Catholic. For this he was disinherited by his
family, and he never returned to the land of his birth.

Winslow continued to enjoy fame and prosperity in the country
of his adoption. He published several books and papers between
1711 and 1742, and left an autobiographical work in manuscript
which was not published until 1912. He married in 1711 Catherine
Gilles, and had a son and a daughter. He lived to the great age
of 91.

Martin Luther (see p. 213).

FOR FURTHER READING

BIOGRAPHIES

ADDISON

Hale-White, W. (1935) *Great Doctors of the Nineteenth Century.* London: Edward Arnold.

BABINSKI

Fulton, J. F. (1933) *J. nerv. ment. Dis.*, 77, 121.

BARTHOLIN

Rhodes, P. (1957) *J. Obstet. Gynæc. Brit. Emp.*, 64, 741.
Speert, H. (1957) *Med. Hist.*, 1, 355.

BELL

Gordon-Taylor, G., and Walls, E. W. (1958) *Sir Charles Bell, His Life and Times.* Edinburgh: E. & S. Livingstone.

BIGELOW

Bigelow, H. S. (1900) *A Memoir of Henry Jacob Bigelow.* Boston: Little, Brown & Co.
Ellis, H. (1969) *A History of Bladder Stone.* Oxford: Blackwell Scientific Publications.

BILLROTH

Rutledge, R. H. (1979) *Surgery*, 5, 672.

BRIGHT

Hale-White, W. (1935) *Great Doctors of the Ninteenth Century.* London: Edward Arnold.

BRODIE

Holmes, T. (1898) *Sir Benjamin Collins Brodie.* ('Masters of Medicine' Series). London: T. Fisher Unwin.

CHARCOT

Tomlinson, J. C., and Haymaker, W. (1957) *Arch. Neurol. Psychiat. (Chicago)*, 77, 44.

CHEYNE

Greenhill, W. A. (1887) *Dict. Nat. Biog.*, 10, 220.
Willius, F. A., and Keys, T. E. (1941) *Cardiac Classics.* London: Kimpton.

CLOQUET

Genty, M. (1933) *Les Biographies Médicales*, 3, 261.

COLLES

Doolin, W. (1958) *Oxford Med. Sch. Gaz.*, *10*, 53.
Widdess, J. D. K. (1949) *A Dublin School of Medicine and Surgery.* Edinburgh: E. & S. Livingstone.

CORRIGAN

Rolleston, H. (1932) *Irish J. med. Sci.*, p. 261.

COURVOISIER

Emrys-Roberts, R. M. (1942) *St. Thos. Hosp. Gaz.*, *40*, 88.

CURIE

Curie, E. (1938) *Madame Curie.* London: Wm. Heinemann.

CUSHING

Fulton, J. F. (1946) *Harvey Cushing. A Biography.* Oxford: Blackwell Scientific Publications.
Stanton, M. E., and Thomson, E. H. (1977) *Surgery*, *81*, 284.
Tilney, N. L. (1980) *Surg. Gynecol. and Obstet.*, *151*, 263.

DOVER

Dewhurst, K. (1947) *The Quicksilver Doctor. The Life and Times of Thomas Dover, Physician and Adventurer.* Bristol: John Wright.

DUPUYTREN

Mondor, H. (1945) *Dupuytren.* Paris: Gallimore.

ERB

Torkildsen, A., and Erickson, T. (1935) *Arch. Neurol. Psychiat. (Chicago)*, *33*, 842.

ESMARCH

Ritter, C. (1908) *Arch. orthop. Unfall-Chir.*, 7, 1.

FALLOPIUS

Singer, C. (1925) *The Evolution of Anatomy.* London: Kegan Paul.
Speert, H. (1955) *Obstet. and Gynec.*, 6, 467.

FERGUSSON

Plarr, V. G. (1930) *Lives of the Fellows of the Royal College of Surgeons of England*, *1*, 398. Bristol: John Wright.

GALEN

Sarton, G. (1954) *Galen of Pergamon.* University of Kansas Press.

GAMGEE

Gamgee, L. P. (1935) *Bgham. med. Rev.*, *10*, 158.

GLAUBER

Hoffmann, K. F. (1955) *Med. Mschr.*, 9, 471.

GRAAF

Catchpole, H. R. (1940) *Bull. Hist. Med.*, 8, 1261.

GRAM

Sonne, C. (1939) *Acta med. scand.*, 98, 441.

GRAVES

Fleetwood, J. (1951) *History of Medicine in Ireland*. Dublin: Browne & Nolan.
Steelhorn, C. E. (1935) *Amer. J. Surg.*, 28, 183.

GRAWITZ

Grote, L. R. (1923) *Die Medizin der Gegenwart in Selbstdarstellungen*, 2, 23. Leipzig: F. Meiner.
Lubasrch, O. (1932) *Virchows Arch. path. Anat.*, 286, 1.

HEBERDEN

Carter, H. S. (1957) *Scot. med. J.*, 480.
Rolleston, H. (1933) *Ann. med. Hist.*, N.S. 5, 409; 566.

HEGAR

Sellheim, H. (1930) *Mschr. Geburtsh. Gynäk.*, 84, 3.

HIPPOCRATES

Chadwick, J., and Mann, W. N. (1950) *The Medical Works of Hippocrates*. Oxford: Blackwell.
Singer, C. (1922) *Greek Biology and Greek Medicine*. Oxford: Clarendon Press.

HIRSCHSPRUNG

Ruhrah, J. (1935) *Amer. J. Dis. Child.*, 50, 472.

HODGKIN

Morrison, H. (1956) *Guy's Hosp. Gaz.*, 70, 358.
Rose, R. (1981) *Curator of the Dead. Thomas Hodgkin (1798–1866)*. London: Peter Owen.

HORSLEY

Lyons, J. B. (1966) *The Citizen Surgeon. A Life of Sir Victor Horsley*, London: Peter Dawnay.
Paget, S. (1919) *Sir Victor Horsley: a Study of His Life and Work*. London: Constable.

HUTCHINSON
Hutchinson, H. (1946) *Jonathan Hutchinson: Life and Letters*. London: Wm. Heinemann Medical Books.

JACKSON
Hale-White, W. (1935) *Great Doctors of the Nineteenth Century*. London: Edward Arnold.
Wilson, S. A. K. (1935) *Lancet, 1*, 882.

KLUMPKE
Jelliffe, S. E. (1928) *Bull. N.Y. Acad. Med., 4*, 655.
Spiller, W. G. (1928) *Arch. Neurol. Psychiat. (Chicago), 20*, 193.

KOCH
Bochalli, R. (1954) *Robert Koch, der Schöpfer der modernen Bakteriologie*. Stuttgart: Wissenschaftliche Verlag.
Brown, L. (1935) *Ann. med. Hist.*, N.S. 7, 99; 292; 385.

KOCHER
Zimmerman, L. M. and Veith, I. (1967) *Great Ideas in the History of Surgery*, 2nd edition. New York: Dover Publications.

KOPLIK
Bass, M. H. (1955) *J. Pediat., 16*, 119.

LANE
Layton, T. B. (1956) *Sir William Arbuthnot Lane, Bt.* Edinburgh: Livingstone.

LISTER
Fisher, R. B. (1977) *Joseph Lister*. London: Macdonald and Jane.
Guthrie, D. (1949) *Lord Lister. His Life and Doctrine*. Edinburgh: Livingstone.

LISTON
Miles, A. (1918) *The Edinburgh School before Lister*. London: A. & C. Black.
Patterson M. J. L. (1958) *St. Barth. Hosp. J., 62*, 135.

LUGOL
Hirsch, A. (1931) *Biographisches Lexikon der hervorragenden Arzte aller Zeiten und Volker, 3*, 863. Berlin: Urban & Schwarzenberg.

McBURNEY
Cope, Z. (1965) *A History of the Acute Abdomen*. London: Oxford University Press.
Preble, E. (1933) *Dict. Amer. Biog., 11*, 555.

MALPIGHI

Richardson, B. W. (1900) *Disciples of Aesculapius*, *1*, 736. London: Hutchinson.

MAYO

Clapesattle, H. (1953) *The Doctors Mayo*, 2nd edition. Minneapolis: University of Minnesota Press.

MECKEL

Beneke, R. (1934) *Johann Friedrich Meckel der Jüngere*. Halle.
Meader, R. G. (1937) *Yale J. Biol. Med.*, *10*, 1.

MENIÈRE

Conde John, F. (1956) *Rev. Laryngol. (Bordeaux)* ¿ *4 1153*.

MOYNIHAN

Bateman, E. (1940) *Berkeley Moynihan, Surgeon*. London: Macmillan.

MURPHY

Davis, L. (1938) *Surgeon Extraordinary: the Life of J. B. Murphy*. London: George G. Harrap.

PAGET

Bett, W. R. (1925) *St. Barth. Hosp. J.*, *33*, 21.
Paget, S. (1902) *Memoirs and Letters of Sir James Paget*. London: Longmans, Green & Co.

PAUL

Power, D'Arcy, and Le Fanu, W. R. (1953) *Lives of the Fellows of the Royal College of Surgeons of England, 1930–1951*. London: Published by the College.

POLITZER

Brühl, G. (1920) *Arch. Ohrenheilk.*, *106*, i.

POTT

Lloyd, S. M. (1933) *St. Barth. Hosp. Rep.*, *66*, 291.

RAMSTEDT

Fischer, I. (1933) *Biographisches Lexikon der hervorragenden Arzte der letzten fünfzig Jahre*, *2*, 1266. Berlin: Urban & Schwarzenberg.

RECKLINGHAUSEN

Councilman, W. T. (1918) *Proc. Amer. Acad. Arts and Sci.*, *53*, 872.
Waldeyer, H. (1910) *Anat. Anz.*, *37*, 509.

REITER

Fischer, I. (1933) *Biographisches Lexikon der hervorragenden Ärzte der letzten fünfzig Jahre, 2*, 1284. Berlin: Urban & Schwarzenberg.

ROBERTSON

Power, D'Arcy. (1912) *Dict. Nat. Biog.*, 2nd Suppl., *3*, 213.

ROENTGEN

Glasser, O. (1945) *Dr. W. C. Röntgen.* Springfield, Illinois: C. C. Thomas.

SIMS

Kelly, H. A. (1935) *Dict. Amer. Biog.*, *17*, 186.
Sims, J. M. (1884) *The Story of My Life.* New York: D. Appleton & Co.

STENSEN

Faller, A. (1957) *Gesnerus*, *14*, 40.
Scherz, G. (1958). *Acta hist. Sci. nat. med.* (Kbh.), *15*, 1–314.

STOKES

Stokes, W. (1898) *William Stokes.* ('Masters of Medicine' Series.) London: T. Fisher, Unwin.

SYME

Paterson, R. (1874) *Memorials of the Life of James Syme.* Edinburgh: Edmonston & Douglas.
Shepherd, J. A. (1969) *Simpson and Syme of Edinburgh.* Edinburgh: Livingstone.

THIERSCH

His, W. (1897–8) *Pop. Sci. Monthly*, *52*, 338.

THOMAS

Le Vay, D. (1956) *The Life of Hugh Owen Thomas.* Edinburgh: E. & S. Livingstone.

VINCENT

Jude, A. (1951) *Bull. Soc. Path. exot.*, *44*, 390.
Tanon, L. (1951) *Bull. Acad. Nat. Méd.*, *135*, 119.

VOLKMANN

Ross, J. P. (1930–1) *St. Barth. Hosp. J.*, *38*, 47.

WASSERMANN

Friedberger, E. (1925) *Z. Immun.-Forsch.*, *43*, i.

WELCH

Flexner, S., and Flexner, J. T. (1941) *William Henry Welch*. New York: Viking Press.

WELLS

Plarr, V. G. (1930) *Lives of the Fellows of the Royal College of Surgeons of England*, 2, 504. Bristol: John Wright.
Shepherd, J. A. (1965) *Spencer Wells. The Life and Work of a Victorian Surgeon*. Edinburgh: Livingstone.

WHARTON

Speert, H. (1956) *Obstet. and Gynec.*, 8, 380.

WIDAL

Astruc, P. (1955) *Progr. méd. (Paris)*, 83, 410.

WILLIS

Richardson, B. W. (1900) *Disciples of Aesculapius*, 1, 592. London: Hutchinson.

WILMS

Trendelenburg, F. (1918) *Dtsch. Z. Chir.*, 145, i.

WINSLOW

Garraud, R. M. (1955) *Presse méd.*, 63, 1589.

FOR GENERAL READING

Cope, Z. (1965) *A History of the Acute Abdomen*. London: Oxford University Press.

Hale-White, W. (1935) *Great Doctors of the Nineteenth Century*. London: Arnold.

Hurwitz, A. and Degenshein, C. A. (1958) *Milestones in Modern Surgery*. New York: Hoeber.

Major, R. H. (1945) *Classic Descriptions of Disease*, 3rd edition. Springfield: Thomas.

Rang, M. (1966) *Anthology of Orthopaedics*. Edinburgh: Livingstone.

Singer, C. and Underwood, E. A. (1962) *A Short History of Medicine*, 2nd edition. Oxford: Clarendon Press.

Zimmerman, L. M. and Veith, I. (1961) *Great Ideas in the History of Surgery*. New York: Dover Publications.

INDEX

264INDEX